Your BOOKSMART, SCHOOL-SAVVY, STRESS-BUSTING PRIMARY TEACHER TRAINING COMPANION

Your BOOKSMART, SCHOOL-SAVVY, STRESS-BUSTING PRIMARY TEACHER TRAINING COMPANION

ELIZABETH MALONE

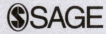

Los Angeles | London | New Delhi
Singapore | Washington DC | Melbourne

Los Angeles | London | New Delhi
Singapore | Washington DC | Melbourne

SAGE Publications Ltd
1 Oliver's Yard
55 City Road
London EC1Y 1SP

SAGE Publications Inc.
2455 Teller Road
Thousand Oaks, California 91320

SAGE Publications India Pvt Ltd
B 1/I 1 Mohan Cooperative Industrial Area
Mathura Road
New Delhi 110 044

SAGE Publications Asia-Pacific Pte Ltd
3 Church Street
#10-04 Samsung Hub
Singapore 049483

Editor: James Clark
Assistant editor: Diana Alves
Production editor: Imogen Roome
Marketing manager: Dilhara Attygalle
Cover design: Naomi Robinson
Typeset by: C&M Digitals (P) Ltd, Chennai, India
Printed in the UK

Library of Congress Control Number: 2019948456

British Library Cataloguing in Publication data

A catalogue record for this book is available from the British Library

ISBN 978-1-5264-9420-7
ISBN 978-1-5264-9419-1 (pbk)

CONTENTS

ABOUT THE AUTHOR

Dr Elizabeth Malone is Head of Primary Initial Teacher Education Programmes at LJMU, where she has taught on a variety of routes for the past ten years. Prior to working at LJMU she worked as a primary teacher, in the UK and abroad, specialising in foreign language education (French and Mandarin). She is passionate about enabling pupils and students to achieve their potential through a commitment to social justice. In her spare time (which is increasingly disappearing due to the increasing numbers of small children in her household) she enjoys participating in sports, from open-water swimming to triathlons, to surfing to bog snorkelling.

ACKNOWLEDGEMENTS

This book is dedicated to our wonderful NHS, without which, for many reasons, this book could not and would not have been written. With particular thanks and an eternal gratitude to all who work in Ward 1C Alder Hey Children's Hospital. Your wisdom, hard work, warmth and compassion knows no limits.

INTRODUCTION

So you are going to be a primary school teacher? Congratulations, it is simply the best job and one of the most important in the entire world. You have the unique opportunity to inspire learners for the rest of their lives. I am often struck that when people at the very top of their profession, be it from sports people to inventors, are interviewed, very frequently they reference the impact on their lives that a single teacher has had. As an illustration, you should Google 'Ian Wright teacher' and I challenge you not to tear up by the end of that video clip. That said, teaching and moreover primary teaching is one of the most misunderstood professions. It would seem that as everyone has been to school everyone feels that they understand it; however, eating at a restaurant is very different from cooking in a kitchen. And so too is teaching in a school rather than attending school.

The multitude of tasks and jobs and roles that you undertake as a primary teacher, each and every day, is hard to explain to your friends and family. Moreover, the general public quite often believe that primary school teaching comprises: playing with kids, lots of holidays and finishing at 3.30 p.m. Of course, these are all 'teaching myths'. Never has there been more accountability and scrutiny in the teaching profession, from all stakeholders including parents, the government and the media. While at the same time, you and your school are expected to operate in increasingly challenging circumstances, including reduced financing while trying to meet the needs of families who are suffering as a result of the cutting of support services. Set against this backdrop, teacher training is a challenging profession to enter into, and perhaps rightly so as you will have the power to inspire or destroy a love of learning for the children whom you will teach. However, there are certain aspects that all student teachers can usually do a little better/less painfully/more time efficiently/all of the above when just shown explicitly how: for example, looking after themselves. And so this book looks to show you just that – the little teacher training life hacks which can make life easier.

Interestingly, as a student teacher you will inhabit two worlds, that of the professional teacher and that of the student. However, recent research has shown that mental health issues for both groups are on the increase; therefore it is paramount you know the common mistakes, how to avoid them and other helpful tips. There are many books on the market which can assist you with your teaching or your studying, however if you yourself are not well and in the 'right place for learning' you can have all the study guides you want, but they will not have an impact. Moreover, if nobody ever explains to you 'why' you should approach a task in a certain way, then it is very difficult to fully get on board with the advice. This book looks to support you to understand why and how to approach all aspects of your teacher training. It does this by dividing each chapter into three useful sections: academic work, placement, and mental health and wellbeing. You can read each chapter in turn, as you progress through your teacher training journey, or you can use the index in the back to dip in and out of sections as they become relevant to you.

The academic work sections look at how you can approach this aspect in the most productive manner. For example, how do you actually go about starting to write an essay? Or what is the best approach to reading? The placement sections are probably a little different from other guides you have been given, although there will be an overlap. This is because this section looks at sharing with you the experiences I have been party to through students, mentors and university tutors over nearly ten years of working in initial teacher education (ITE). Consider it a peek 'behind the curtain'. For example, how to overcome 'imposter syndrome' (Clance and Imes, 1978) is an interesting section as it is such a common feeling among trainee teachers, while the mental health and wellbeing sections consider how you can stay well while training to teach. Happy people make happy teachers; and happy teachers are good teachers.

This book is not aimed at one particular age group or training route of teachers. This is because the issues that trainee teachers come across and experience are not split in this way. In any cohort, the same themes and questions arise. As such the book has an in-depth consideration of several groups of students who may be looking for specific guidance, such as the 'busy working parent' or LGBT students. The book seeks to answer those questions about training to be a teacher that you would not feel comfortable asking in university or in school, but do need to be explored. Consider this book your friendly aunty guide to teacher training. A book that contains a reassuring message, which after a long day at school or university you can brew up and start to read, realising that a) you are not alone (in fact what you are experiencing is very, very normal, whatever it is); b) there is a solution; and c) you can and will overcome the hurdle and become a successful teacher.

Your journey into teaching and along your teaching career will be an interesting one and of your own making. You can choose to be inventive, ask questions and break the mould. You can also choose to emulate fantastic teaching you have seen. You could do one of these on a Monday morning and by the afternoon have adopted a whole different style. What I am trying to say is that you will, as they say, never get bored. Although, when teaching Class X on a rainy Thursday after-noon, in deepest darkest November, with several academic essays due in, this might be a state of affairs you find yourself wishing for.

Get curious, get inspiring and get teaching. And the best of luck with it. To quote Dr. Seuss (1990), 'And will you succeed? Yes! You will, indeed! (98 and 3/4 percent guaranteed.)' But before you get carried away, do take the time to read the rest of this book so you don't make it harder than it needs to be.

1

- the different teaching approaches and the importance of questioning everything
- what is imposter syndrome and how to overcome it to become your best self while on placement
- different ways that you can organise yourself.

ACADEMIC

GETTING STARTED

The academic aspect of teaching training is very much the 'ugly sister' to 'Cinderella' placements. After all, presumably you took up the offer to join a teacher training course because you want to make a positive impact on the lives of learners and not to sit in lecture theatres. You took up the offer of teacher training because you want to do something. You have some ideas, and as Dr. Seuss says, 'You have brains in your head. You have feet in your shoes. You can steer yourself any direction you choose. You're on your own. And you know what you know. And *you* are the one who'll decide where to go ...'. Then, you find yourself captured, placed in a room and asked to discuss educational approaches, interpret research- and evidence-informed teaching, and draw links from this for your classroom teaching. This isn't how you planned to make a difference. You do not want to be doing this. You want to be out there, at the coalface making a difference, learning from experienced professional teachers in schools. How, then, can you be convinced of the importance of attending university sessions and become excited about this prospect?

It may help to consider whether you view teaching as a profession, a trade or a craft. It may be that teaching straddles all of these approaches. However, given that teaching is one of the most important jobs, without it there would be no other future jobs, an expected understanding of research- and evidence-based enquiry is a reasonable starting place. Moreover, quite often, this is the area trainee teachers need to develop first. There is an argument that by learning these critical analysis skills, a teacher will continue to develop even when in post. Furthermore, developing these skills will help to 'futureproof' you against the next teaching 'fad'.

What is a teaching fad? Well, a good example for this is what is known as the 'neuromyth' of learning styles, more commonly known as VAK (visual, audio, kinaesthetic). However, it is important to note that one of the problems with this approach is that actually there is no clear, agreed framework, nor definition of what 'learning styles' are. The general belief seems to be that pupils have a preferred way of learning and that providing information to them in this style would help to best cater for their needs. Critics have raised the concern that following this approach may lead pupils to have a fixed mindset about how they learn or may hamper their ability to adapt. Furthermore, the Educational Endowment Foundation (see Chapter 6 for further details) has concluded that learning styles as a teaching approach is 'low impact for very low cost, based on limited evidence'. While on one hand the cost implications are low in terms of not having to buy equipment or textbooks, on the other hand if teachers are spending their planning, preparation and assessment (PPA) time engaged in creating a VAK approached planning for all children and the resources to go with it, it could be suggested that for time-scarce teachers VAK comes at quite a high cost. Finally, the low-impact status coupled with limited evidence is really quite damning. Through developing criticality and becoming informed about a variety of approaches to learning when you become a teacher you will be better placed to really consider new schemes and approaches which are 'sold' to teachers and explore their educational underpinnings before making a decision to follow a set approach. You may in fact decide that one set approach is not for you, and you may decide that you wish to gather all of your knowledge and craft your own teaching style, for the specific needs of the pupils in your class. Therefore, while it is understandable that maybe the academic aspect of your teacher training does not make you as excited as your placement does, it is still an important part of your overall development as a professional teacher. It is just more of what could be described as 'a slow burn'.

There can be a real desire from trainee teachers, particularly at the start of a course, to learn about what could be described as 'tips for teachers'. Tips for teachers are handy, bite-sized suggestions of activities or tasks that you can do with your pupils in school. These tips are usually really exciting and enjoyable tasks, with great resources, or perhaps they are easily applicable ideas such as behaviour charts or formative assessment ideas. These ideas or tips are easy to remember and easy to apply as all the heavy lifting (e.g. the planning of the approach) has been done for you. This means that at the beginning of a course, when you may have little experience and little knowledge from which to craft your own ideas, you can easily get up and running in the classroom. However, these approaches have a short shelf life. This is because without an understanding of the theoretical underpinnings and ideas, which support these tips, you may find that you are unable to adapt them to meet the specific needs of your class. Furthermore, there may be times when these tips are not actually suitable for the needs of your particular class. In addition, this is where your university sessions will come into their own. They provide you with firm foundations from which you can plan your personalised teaching approach for each class that you teach. It is not that there is anything wrong with 'tips for teachers'; these can be helpful in providing you with ideas and things to try out in your class. However, there is a time and a place for them, and it is useful to understand their limitations. If you like, 'tips for teachers' could be considered 'fast food', pre-packaged, easy and convenient, while university could be considered your vegetables, not too sexy, good for you and requiring a little work to make it edible.

Uni = vegetables

TRAINEE TEACHERS WITH ADDITIONAL NEEDS

Trainee teachers come in many delightful forms. For some this is their first experience of leaving home and going to university, some are recent graduates, while others are returning to university following a period of work. As a varied bunch of people, there are a number of different student needs; for example, some students may have dyslexia or dyspraxia, others may be on the autistic spectrum, some have caring responsibilities or may be experiencing mental health issues and some may have a variety of needs.

Having an additional need can make a trainee teacher feel vulnerable, particularly depending on previous experiences, and it is important to ensure that you get the support that you need from the start. For some trainee teachers this may already be in place, and so while they work harder, just to keep pace with their cohort, they do not feel ready to share their additional needs with schools or university. Of course, this is fine; no one is under any obligation to disclose his or her additional needs. However, you may find that it is useful if you do, as there are some forms of additional support which can be put in place for you. For example, this could be an assignment extension or, if you have a specific need plan, you may be entitled to some one-to-one support. Some students start their courses with Individual Student Learning Plans (ISLPs) from previous institutions or courses although they do not yet have one for their teacher training courses. It can be useful for your tutors and programme leaders to have a copy of the previous plan (as long as you are comfortable in sharing) while you wait for your new plan. This means that they can make any adjustments that they might need to for you. It might be worth considering assignment extensions at this point. Most university module leaders will have a discretional number of days that they can provide you with, should you have additional needs or perhaps have been affected by another life event which has prevented you from handing work in on time. They will also be able to provide you with a longer extension but you may need to provide 'evidence' such as a medical evidence. However, extensions are not always useful on a busy teacher training courses. When your programme was created, time will have been spent organising and arranging where and when you will hand in your assignments, and this will have been planned to avoid crunch times for you. If you come to rely on extensions this can cause other jobs and assignments to mount up, which really is not helpful. Ideally, if you do have additional needs, which you need support with, it would be good practice to try to address issues you might have earlier rather than later. For example, if you know that you struggle with organising your thoughts for academic work, rather than waiting until close to the deadline date and then asking for an extension, you could try to arrange support in creating a plan of attack when you first receive the assignment briefing. Of course, extensions are there as a safety blanket, and sometimes even with the best intentions students may end up needing them, and this is completely fine. These things and life do happen, and an extension is better than a non-submission.

If you do find yourself in a situation where you are not going to complete an assignment on time and have also been denied an extension then you should submit whatever work you have done so far, no matter how incomplete. This is because what you do submit will be marked and you will gain feedback on what you have done so far. This is important as it means that you can use this feedback when you come to rewrite your next piece. If you simply do not submit, there is nothing to mark and thus you will not receive any insights.

Trainee teachers with additional needs also face the choice of whether or not to disclose their needs while on placement. Alas, again, there is no right answer here; this has to be personal choice. Most schools are fantastic at proving support and making accommodations, if they know there are additional needs. As you are usually working in close proximity for a prolonged period, your school may get a sense that 'something is up' and not be able to fully understand what is going on. For example, if you are a dyslexic student you will need to develop a series of strategies to support yourself while on placement. One of these may be concerned with spellings. There are a couple of approaches you could take: you could ensure that you have key spellings in your planning or on the board ready to go and you may also choose to model how to look up spelling for your pupils. If you have chosen to disclose on placement then this is where your class teacher or teaching assistant (TA) could also act as a 'backstop' and let you know if you have made a particular spelling mistake. Another example might be if you are undergoing counselling for a particular mental health condition your school may arrange for you to take your PPA at this time to enable you to make your appointment and then catch up with planning later when you return.

If you do decide to disclose your additional needs in school, do make sure that you try to set aside time to do this properly, such as during a weekly meeting. This is because, if you simply reveal that you have an additional need in the form of a label or term, your mentor's experience with this need previously could very much influence the outcomes of the support you receive. It can be better to highlight what your needs are and what sort of support you would welcome, and when you would find this useful. In this way, you can inform your school about your needs and how they affect you personally, ensuring that you receive the help and support that you would welcome, when you need it. Your mentor may have questions, which they may feel embarrassed to ask, feeling that perhaps they should already know the answers. If you sense that this is the case, a useful question can be to ask, 'Have I explained this OK?' (this works really well when working with children too). This is because by phrasing the question in this way, you can remove feelings that they should already know about your condition, by moving the emphasis on to you.

CASE STUDY 1.1   ADDITIONAL NEEDS

Betsy had worked in a bank prior to starting the teacher training course and had a toddler. At the start of the course she progressed well; however, as the teaching expectation increased and the workload became heavier, she started to struggle. She would often arrive

(Continued)

at school just moments before the children and was unprepared. On a university visit to her placement, her files were checked and were found to be missing many required aspects while her planning was a particular cause for concern. Her initial teacher training (ITT) mentor and her university tutor had a discussion with Betsy about what was causing her to fall behind and to what she allocated her time. Betsy said that her planning took a long time, but when this was looked at in closer detail, some plans were missing and many were sparse. Betsy then went to a new placement and it was hoped that she would have a fresh start, but after an initial two weeks of progress, the same issues started to emerge. Her tutors met with her again to see if support could be put into place for Betsy, but she repeated that there was nothing that could be done, as she did not require any support. Her tutors wondered what could be affecting her progress; they discussed a whole raft of possibilities, including if becoming a parent had been a difficult transition for Betsy, if her family supported her, if she had the organisational skills to participate in the course and even if she had the commitment to the training course. Eventually, through lack of progression, Betsy was placed on the university's additional support framework, and again repeatedly failed to make progress. It was at this point that her tutors assumed (incorrectly as it happens) that Betsy was a) not capable of making the required progress and b) not committed to the course as she repeatedly failed to engage with university services and her placement.

Having eventually failed two of her placements, Betsy's options were very limited. It was at this point that Betsy revealed that she had recently found out that she was at risk of a genetic, heritable disease, which if she were a carrier would not only affect her, but the lives of her children too. She had been caring for her elderly mother, who had also recently been placed in a home, but only after a prolonged stay with Betsy. Betsy had been waking in the night not only to look after her toddler but her mother as well. On occasion, her mother had gone missing, meaning that Betsy could be late or not able to work in the evenings. Betsy had made the decision to not find out if she was a genetic carrier for the disease; however, when she met two of her cousins in town, they revealed to her that they were carriers. When Betsy explained this to her tutors it completely reframed Betsy's behaviour and clarified why she had acted and performed as she had.

Her tutors were regretful that they had not known, and had not been able to support her, while Betsy was not sure why she had not revealed her situation. After this, she was given another placement and, through a package of support, she passed the course. Of course, not everyone's situation is as serious or life threatening as Betsy's, but more often than not trainee teachers overestimate their ability to keep private and professional lives separate. As teacher training courses are often busy and at times stressful, if you are experiencing a difficult time or you have additional needs which are not being met then this can all add to the stress and at times 'leak' out. The chances are that your school or tutor will not be able to pinpoint exactly what is wrong, but might have a 'spidey sense' that something is not quite right, so it can be helpful for all to chat about it and be in the know. However, it is important to reiterate that this is a decision that only you can make and as such should be one that you feel comfortable with.

PLACEMENT

INTRODUCTIONS

Imposter Syndrome

Starting at a new place of work can be daunting. Starting at a new place of work with the label 'trainee' is positively cruel. This is because you can feel quite exposed in front of the teachers and the pupils in the school. This feeling can be further compounded if you are one of the teachers who ends up on placement in the school that they attended as a child. Therefore, this section looks at explicitly considering why you might lack confidence going into a school and offers practical suggestions for what you can do to ensure a good start to the year.

Some trainee teachers may experience what is known as imposter syndrome. Imposter syndrome was first coined by Clance and Imes (1978) and can be explained as the feeling of being an 'intellectual phoney'. This means that, irrespective of academic qualifications or other achievements, those 'who experience the imposter phenomenon persist in believing that they are really not bright and have fooled anyone who thinks otherwise. Numerous achievements, which one might expect to provide ample objective evidence of superior intellectual functioning, do not appear to affect the impostor belief' (Clance and Imes, 1978: 1). While imposter syndrome can affect anyone, it predominately affects women, which is interesting as the vast majority of teachers are women, and only 38 per cent of secondary and 15 per cent of primary teachers are males (DfE, 2016). Therefore, the chances are that you are a female who research shows is more affected by imposter syndrome or perhaps you are a male teacher in a predominately female environment, which could also create feelings of not belonging. So, for example, you may already feel like you do not belong on a teacher training course, that by some fluke you have managed to 'bluff your way through the interview, and trick your way on to the course and that sooner or later you're going to get found out, 'cos you're not really supposed to be here or a teacher'. These feelings are compounded when learning to teach because this is a 'performance sport', which has to be conducted in public and to an audience of your pupils and usually your mentor. Moreover, this process requires you to learn by doing and then receive feedback. However, if you have internalised feelings of being an imposter, it can be really difficult to muster the strength and courage to get up and teach in the first place, let alone be in a good place to receive constructive feedback without concentrating on the negatives (see Chapter 3, 'Thinking about thoughts'). Finally, it may be that the ITT mentor you are working with or the headteacher of your school also feels like an 'intellectual phoney'. This may be hard for you to believe, as they are usual much more qualified than you are, with much more experience, but this is where imposter syndrome (IM) does not discriminate. It is not a feeling based in reality, or grounded in evidence; in fact it is more the opposite. A common example, which can affect trainee teachers, is when they ask to see what their class teacher is planning and this is refused. Generally, this can be because the class teacher is anxious or worried about being judged, or may feel that by sharing their work they will be 'exposed' as a phoney. There really is not much that, as a trainee, you can do about this; however, it is often helpful to try to understand the mindsets of others, because if you understand their motivations it can make a difference. To illustrate, there is a large difference between the teacher who does not want to share his/her planning because they do not want to help you and the teacher who cannot bring themselves to share his/her planning because they are terrified this will expose them finally as a poor teacher who should not be there. You are still in the same situation (without any planning). However, in one situation you might be a little miffed, creating tension in your relationship. In the other scenario, perhaps you are a little more understanding.

Clance and Imes (1978: 1) state that imposter syndrome does not affect 'any one diagnostic category'. However, the 'clinical symptoms most frequently reported are generalized anxiety, lack of self-confidence, depression, and frustration related to inability to meet self-imposed standards of achievement'. This last consideration is interesting, because trainee teachers often set themselves incredibly high standards to meet and some can exhibit perfectionist traits. Unfortunately, there will always be something to learn or something to do in the field of teaching and learning and so being perfect is not really an end option. This can cause anxiety and stress for some teachers, further perpetuating the feeling of being an imposter and heightening the fear of 'being found out', either by their school mentor, the pupils in the class or perhaps the parents of the children whom they are teaching.

So what can we do about feeling like an imposter in school? Well, one of the first things is just to be aware of this syndrome, and if you feel, having read this section, that this could indeed be you, then do conduct some further reading. Clance and Imes (1978) recommend group therapy, which might be a little difficult for you to arrange; however, it might be worthwhile speaking about this experience with a group of friends on your teacher training course and finding out how your friends see you. One of your friends will no doubt be able to see you objectively, simply will have no understanding of how you see yourself and will hopefully be able to mirror this back to you as based on the 'evidence', e.g. your brilliant grades, fantastic teaching observations and numerous leisure achievements. Clance and Imes also recommend that you keep a record of positive feedback and note this all down. The chances are that your mind will only remember the negative feedback you have received. This is all part of your freeze, flight or fight mechanism for keeping you safe, which your brain has evolved to keep track of the 'issues' in case it is called upon to do something with this information. However, your brain has not quite updated itself to today's lives and, as such, there is no immediate danger; however, your brain is still operating in this way. So try to keep a log of all the positive comments, from pupils, TAs, mentors and parents, and in this way you will have 'evidence' of your reasons to be there.

There are also biochemical hacks, which can help you to feel more confident when going into school and learning how to teach. One of the most helpful sets of practical applications comes from Amy Cuddy (2012) who is a social psychologist. Her research is interesting for a number of reasons, but perhaps the most important is the finding that how you sit or stand can affect how you feel. It is reasonably well understood that the inverse is true, e.g. how you feel affects your body language. However, this is a two-way street. In Cuddy's research (do take twenty minutes to watch her TED talk on this topic), she found that 'powerful poses' such as arms open, chest out, legs spread, hands on hips (think 'open' body, like a great big ape) increase testosterone and lower cortisol. Testosterone (think of this as the confidence hormone) and cortisol (consider this the stress hormone) both contribute to our feelings of confidence and power. The inverse is also true, so 'shy/scared' poses, such as arms crossed, small gestures, eyes down, slumped shoulders (think trying to be as small as possible), produce less testosterone and more cortisol. If you are learning how to teach and always receiving feedback, it is going to feel different depending on how you are feeling, so you need to give

47 ↓ C = mindful of poses.

yourself a fighting chance to start with. You could try to bust out some large shapes in the loo before you teach and be mindful of your body language so you can try to boost your testosterone and lower your cortisol. This will make you feel more confident and hopefully put you in a better position mentally/emotionally to take teaching risks and engage openly and honestly with feedback.

Another helpful strategy to consider when learning to teach is to audit what you are good at and then offer to provide some leadership in this area for your school. For example, if you are great at knitting, tennis or bird watching you could offer to run a club for the pupils in your school. If your talents lie within a specific area of the curriculum, let the leader in the area know and offer to help with curriculum developments. It's important that as well as learning in a school you can also contribute to the school. This will help to make you an integral part of the school community, moving you from being 'that trainee' to 'the teacher who helps with [insert your own area here]', and it will also help you because you will be able to maximise strengths that you have.

Your first interactions with pupils in schools could be compared with going to prison. In jail, many prisoners will size up other inmates the minute that they walk through the door and then they make a decision on how to treat them. Now, this is where we will leave this illustration because the decisions that prisoners make and the decisions pupils make are very different. For your pupils, in the main, they decide on three possible routes: to toe the line, to experiment and see what they can get away with or to cause mayhem with you from day one. Forewarned is forearmed, and as such you should really do your groundwork first. Have a good read of the school website, try to get in touch with your class teacher prior to starting and become aware of any children with particular needs, and of course read your school's policies (see Chapter 2 on behaviour management). However, you can also do some simple things like making sure that you dress appropriately within the school, ensuring that you are set up and ready to go with minimum fuss, and following school polices to ensure that you are part of a much bigger organism.

Finally, in busy schools trainee teachers can sometimes get a little bit lost. That said, tins of biscuits never, ever get lost. It may be a nice idea on your first day to take in a box of sweet treats and a little card, which introduces you to the staff. You can leave it on the table, and as people come and go they can read it over and have a treat. This is a nice way to introduce yourself, outlining why you are there, for how long, what you are looking forward to (choose something from the website which has impressed you, the more personalised the better) and what you wish to contribute to the school while you are there. Lastly, when you leave, you can do the same, but with a thank you card.

Also contribute to the school eg running fitness

MENTAL HEALTH AND WELLBEING

INFORMATION OVERLOAD: HOW TO PRIORITISE AND BE ORGANISED

When you start a teaching course, you will be given a huge amount of information all at once. You will be given placement information, academic arrangements, essay briefings, timetables, Teacher's Standards, files for placement, files for evidencing QTS (qualified teacher status), files for developing your subject knowledge, reading lists and handouts in sessions. By the end of your first term, the concept of a paperless society will make you laugh out loud, as you realise that, as far as teaching is concerned, physical paper is very much in charge. So then, what's the plan for all this stuff and why do you need it anyway? All good questions that we will have a look at below.

Of course, the problem with receiving information at the start of anything is that you do not really need it then. At the start of a teaching course, you are very much focused on how you are going to be the most inspiring teacher that ever lived. How the kids in your class are going to love you because you are different, you are [choose your own adjective here] funny/musical/weird/environmentally conscious/a Jedi. The last thing you want to read is a module guide or an assessment-marking grid. Moreover, this is fine, and completely reasonable. However, the secret is to create some sort of system, so that you

Create a system :

can find the information again when it is relevant, furthermore a system which works when you have long forgotten that you actual have information about a topic.

Simply put, you are going to have to make an investment in a number of stationery items. You can try to go paperless, which is a commendable approach. However, the teaching world just does not seem to have updated itself yet so there is simply no other alternative to the purchasing of ring-binder files.

You should have a file for university information, and at least one file for placement. Many students as per the recommendations of their university will have a subject knowledge file, a classroom file and an evidencing QTS file. It might be worth considering each one of these because students can often misplace their time working on tasks that actually are just paperwork for paperwork's sake rather than contributing to making you a better teacher.

The subject knowledge file will contain 'evidence' of how you have developed your subject knowledge. Printing off handouts and copying from books does not necessarily impact on your teaching and therefore the learning of your pupils. Quite often one of the best places that you can be to develop your subject knowledge can be in the classes with the pupils. This is because, presumably, you are lacking the subject knowledge to teach and, as such, it follows that when this is being taught to the pupils it can be useful for you to be in there. In a similar approach, it can also be useful to attend the lessons in other year groups in the same topics, and then you can see the progression in the subject. A word of caution about observations of experienced teachers teaching, if you go into a class and try to observe everything, you will in fact come out with nothing. This is because when you watch an experienced professional teach, it looks like magic, and much of what they are doing is 'hidden' in either their preparation, planning or assessment approaches. Therefore, it can be useful to just hone in on one or two specific standards, really try to unpick what you are seeing and if possible ask the teacher about their motivation to take a particular decision. It may be that your university provides you with an observation form, which contains empty boxes to be completed for all of the standards. However, it might be worth a discussion with your university lecturers to see if there is indeed the requirement to populate all of these boxes. Trainee teachers can also sometimes lose sight of the end goal of tasks. You are developing your subject knowledge to have an impact in the classroom, rather than just to know more. As such, a good way of logging what you have learned can be to use your lesson plans, which demonstrate what you have learned regarding a topic and an approach. That said, a lesson plan is

TIP

just that: a plan. You may find that what you set out to teach and what the pupils actually learned may be on some occasions different. Therefore, you should also look to include your evaluations and lesson analysis forms too.

A classroom file is an interesting one as this will differ the most between all trainees. It may be that your university or school gives you a huge, mega list of things to put into this file, in which case creating this file is really quite boring and easy – you simply follow the list. If you are not given guidance about this file, it won't be because your university doesn't care, but more simply that as a 'squatter' in someone else's classroom it might be best to agree with your class teacher what they would like you to have in this file. Your classroom file should contain all information pertaining to the teaching and learning in your class. If you are ever absent, your class teacher should be able to access this file and see what you had planned previously, how the children got on and any other information. It will also contain information for you such as groupings, assessments and maybe seating plans. Some of the information about your class will be personal or sensitive data and, as such, you should ensure that names are anonymised and individual children cannot be identified.

The final file that you might have is an evidencing QTS file. In order to pass your course you must show that you meet the Teachers' Standards. Let us now stop to consider the Teachers' Standards and what they are focused on. Well, the answer is the teaching and more importantly the learning. Just simply developing you and your teaching is a misdirection. You are developing your teaching to meet the needs of the learners in your class. Meeting the Teachers' Standards does not exist in a vacuum on one side, while you do all your teaching and learning in another area. In fact, quite the opposite is true. Your teaching and learning *is* meeting the Teachers' Standards. As such, it follows that everything you do, as you go about your general teachery-ness, is evidence for the Teachers' Standards. You do not need to manufacture witness statements, for example, because in your normal day-to-day teacher role you will be writing lessons plans, evaluating and being observed, and all of these things that you generate will be your evidence. Each year trainees obsess about 'evidence' when actually everything you do evidences the Standards. Eventually, many realise that they can use their weekly meeting forms, review forms and lesson analysis of their teaching but are surprised to learn that they can use their own lesson plans or evaluations of their own teaching.

Certainly, when you start teaching you will be mentored and provided with more assistance and, as such, you may rely more heavily on the opinion of others. However, eventually you need to move from being mentored to being coached, and this means developing your own reflective practice so you can make your own judgements about your teaching and take steps to improve. Sometimes the inverse is just as important: you realise when your teaching has gone well and why, so you can look to do this again, and also feel proud of your accomplishments. Therefore, a QTS file will simply house all of the other paperwork which you cannot house elsewhere, such as review forms or subject knowledge audits. Some trainees divide their QTS file into each of the eight Standards. This is a bad idea. Not only does it become unwieldy, but also you end up with a huge admin load as you are photocopying items so that they can go into different sections. It would be better to simply log your 'evidence' in its natural place and keep a standards log of where the information is housed, a sort of breadcrumb trail to find where it has been filed. Now, of course, you should always follow the recommendations of your university and school, because ultimately they will be awarding you QTS. However, it is hoped that this section has demystified some of the approaches and requirements, which can tangle students up in knots.

Now that we have dealt with the files, it might be useful to consider 'Parkinson's Law'. This law states that work expands to fill the time available for its completion. As a trainee teacher you will have many plates to keep spinning, and as such one of the key skills you can learn is how to break down a task into its component pieces, to work backwards on a calendar putting in each little component piece every week, and to allocate an appropriate amount of time to each job. This will then ensure that you are on task and on time with all of your jobs. Of course, anyone who has ever seen *Grand Designs* knows that sometimes (well, all the time on *Grand Designs*) they will, despite great and detailed project plans, go both over time and over budget. Things and life do happen, so try not to worry. However, if you do have a little 'slippage' you can be guaranteed it will be more insignificant than if you had not had a plan in the first place. Let us look at an example. If you have to create a unit of work ready for the start of your next placement, consider the component pieces you need to break it down into. Well, you'll need to know the class's needs, prior needs, topic and end outcome. Then you may need to research your subject knowledge. Sharing this plan before the date with your ITT mentor to check you are on the 'right lines' might be useful. Then you have to create the plan and make any resources. At this point, you are probably rolling your eyes. Of course, you know this, but it does not mean that you do it. Everyone knows they should eat vegetables, some fruit and get exercise each day, but few people actually do this. So bear with me. The reason why breaking down tasks is important is because if you have purchased a diary, a wall planner and a to-do-list you are almost half way there. However, if you then put in your diary and to-do-list 'plan unit of work', when you sit down to action this you will not be able to do so. Instead, you will sit at your desk frustrated because you need to do some groundwork (prior learning, etc.) before you can start. Furthermore some of these jobs may need to be done in school, and the time you have allocated to starting this job is an evening or week-end. However, if you have really broken a job down, you can start to attack little tasks prior to tackling the 'main job'. This means you will work more efficiently and quickly. A classic sign that the jobs you are setting yourself are far too 'big' and need to be broken down are that the same jobs roll over, day after day, and week after week. This approach takes a little time, but once you get to grips with it, it can be enormously helpful, not just for training but also when teaching.

When I used to teach, I taught one-to-one tuition as part of a school's Pupil Premium funding. I would often try to engage the pupils in their learning, through asking questions about motivation and engagement. Generally, the children would tell me that they had not done something (e.g. homework, task in class) because it was boring. I would then ask them if it was OK to be bored. Of all the children asked, 100 per cent said firmly no, it was not OK to be bored. In fact, it is OK to be bored. It certainly is not an enjoyable state, and really it would be better if the learning your children were engaged in was interesting or motivating, but sometimes it is OK to be bored. You may be wondering where is this going. The same concept applies to you and your work. Agreed, it would be much better if you were not bored, but sometimes you simply have to engage with a task, which is a little dull, and this is OK. However, you do have a choice: you can lengthen the time a boring task takes up of your life by allowing your mind and fingers to wan-der over to more interesting elements of the Internet, or you can try to develop a working mindset. If there is no other option than to do the task you do not want to do, a good approach is to get it out of the way first and every time you are tempted to spend time elsewhere on different things, remember that in the long run you are actually prolonging your misery. Don't do this to yourself. Again, as with everything in life, you'll need to practise this. You may find that before you know it you are shopping online or watching some funny video, and if you catch yourself doing this, just gen-tly remind yourself of what needs to be done and why. Occasionally, if you have been working on a prolonged task such as an academic essay, you may find that task switching is helpful. Through this approach, instead of giving up and stopping work, you might find that it's helpful to change what you are doing and it gives you a little boost before eventually returning to the original task with fresh eyes.

In terms of helping to organise you and your workload, once you have bro-ken down the tasks, your smartphone is one of the most helpful devices you can use to support yourself. You can programme your phone with a variety of alarms and reminders to help to ensure that you finish all of your jobs in time and that tasks do not sneak up on you. A word of caution, this approach is only as good as the programming that you input. Trainees often overlook their university email account, as this can be considered a passé medium of communication. Unfortunately, unless your lecturer knocks on all of your houses and comes in to tell you your information, or makes phone calls to you all, this is the only option that they have to share information. Do make sure that either you have your emails linked up to your phones or you get into the habit of checking your emails regularly.

There are of course a number of publications that discuss prioritising, organisation and managing workload in much greater detail than could ever be covered here. Trial and error will help you to create your very own blend of approaches. However, it is hoped that this section provides a different perspective and helps you to see your tasks differently, placing them within a larger concept of impact on learning for the pupils whom you teach.

CHAPTER SUMMARY

- Question everything and do your own reading. Don't accept glossy Pinterest lists and Instagram posts and DfE latest recommendations as your teaching approach. Who is informing you? What have they based their suggestions on? What are their biases? Get informed.
- Accept that 'getting informed' takes time.
- Communicate with everyone: on placement, at home, at university. Everything is totally solvable, and little things are easier to fix earlier.
- Be friendly. Be authentic. Be you. Well you know, unless you're a complete narcissistic nut job, in which case, probably best to be someone else. If in doubt, take in biscuits.
- Fake it, until you become it.
- Get organised. Really organised. Totally organised and then a little bit more organised.
- Do the little jobs *every day*. That way little jobs don't ever become big jobs you cannot face.
- Don't be a busy fool, or a performative teacher. Consider if what you are spending your time doing will make you or your children's learning better; if not, don't waste your time.

TIP

FURTHER READING

Clance, P. R. and Imes, S. A. (1978) 'The imposter phenomenon in high achieving women: Dynamics and therapeutic intervention', *Psychotherapy: Theory, Research & Practice*, 15(3): 241–247. http://dx.doi.org/10.1037/h0086006.

This is a link to Clance and Imes' original work, from which you can start to explore the concept of imposter syndrome. Those identifying as male, please don't be put off by the title. The work contains something for everyone and, as suggested above, as a male in a predominately female profession, you will most probably be able to identify with the concept well.

Cuddy, A. (2012) 'Your body may shape who you are'. www.ted.com/talks/amy_cuddy_your_body_language_shapes_who_you_are?language=en (accessed 2 September 2019).

This is a 20-minute talk which introduces you to Amy Cuddy's research from 2012. She received some criticisms for her work, which she went on to refute and so it is also worth reading the *Forbes* article by Kim Elsesser.

Elsesser, K. (2018) 'Power posing is back: Amy Cuddy successfully refutes criticism', *Forbes*, 3 April. www.forbes.com/sites/kimelsesser/2018/04/03/power-posing-is-back-amy-cuddy-successfully-refutes-criticism/ (accessed 2 September 2019).

McKay, B. and McKay, K. (2018) 'How to quit mindlessly surfing the Internet and actually get stuff done', *The Art of Manliness*, 6 December. www.artofmanliness.com/articles/how-to-quit-mindlessly-surfing-the-internet-and-actually-get-stuff-done/ (accessed 2 September 2019).

Having advocated for research-informed, evidence-based sources, I'm about to ignore this recommendation, and point you towards an Internet source of questionable 'gravitas'. It is further compounded by being part of a dubiously named website, 'The art of manliness'. However, all of these issues acknowledged, the two authors (Brett and Kate McKay) detail, in step-by-step guidance, hacks to ensure that you remain focused on your tasks, instead of mindlessly surfing the Internet, from the 'nuclear option' (blocking all the timewasting sites from your laptop) to other gentler suggestions. It's worth a read, but you will also need to implement the techniques if you wish to see results.

2

ACADEMIC READING, CLASSROOM BEHAVIOUR AND BEING KIND TO YOURSELF

- the importance of reading before you start writing
- getting to know your children and how to approach behaviour
- how to be kind to yourself and recognise that you won't know everything from the beginning.

ACADEMIC

READING: HOW TO READ AND WHY BOTHER

This section will consider 'reading'. (It is in inverted commas because there is a vast array of interesting other forms of gaining knowledge these days, e.g. podcasts – see Chapter 6 which offers more ideas.) It will also explore why reading is an integral part of any learning experience. It will look at different forms of reading and consider critical literacy skills such as which sources are suitable and which should be considered with a 'pinch of salt'. Not all online platforms are equal.

On a teacher training course you will be expected to supplement your time in sessions with additional reading, and your course will often have a number of recommended texts. It is quite common for students to overlook these reading lists, but they really should act as a starting point for all students. You will be expected to read books and journal articles, although increasingly lecturers are recommending videos and podcasts as supplementary forms of literature. Before we start to look at the different types of reading and how each of these might be useful, it is worth stopping to consider what the main differences are between these different types of publications. Journal articles will be more 'current' as it takes less time to publish an article than the average two years it takes to have a book published. However, you will tend to find that journal articles can be quite 'niche': sometimes considering small sample sizes and particular research questions, which may or may not be relevant to your particular situation in

Journals
pros/
cons.

school. Finally, Internet websites, videos and podcasts need to be critically appraised for their value. You should always bear in mind that journal articles have to be peer reviewed to be published, and books have to go through several editorial checks, but the Internet allows the self-publication of materials. Don't throw the baby out with the bath water and disregard everything you read online. Instead, if something catches your eye, see if you can search for the same ideas using journal articles or books and then follow the research thread from there.

Let us now look at what could be consider to be the five main types of reading: Google booking, skimming, scanning, intensive and extensive. Each can be of use to the busy trainee teacher.

GOOGLE BOOKING

Google Books has revolutionised how essays are now written. Once upon a time, tired students had to make the long journey to a physical library. There they would look through the Dewey Decimal System for the books they would need, or trudge over to the stacks (large metal containers with journals in them) and sift through the editions. However, while looking for their actual items a student might stumble across another text or see another journal article, which looked interesting, pick this up and become informed about a topic they had no previous knowledge of. Alas, Google Books means some students are now are less informed than previously. This is because instead of a student reading widely and then writing an essay from the ideas which they have read, said student can write an essay out of ideas which are already in their head, then go to Google Books to google a reference to 'add in' to 'back up' a point. This means that key ideas can often be missed, the level of criticality of the essay is shallow and the student really has not learned as much as they could have done while writing the essay. This is not to suggest that you should boycott Google Books, just that there are different ways in which you could consider using it instead. By making an informed choice to use Google Books as the first in a series of actions (e.g. combined with some of the approaches below), rather than last in the writing process, you'll find that not only are your essays better but you are more informed.

SKIMMING

Skimming is simply casting your eye over an article or text, looking for key terms or phrases to enable deeper reading later. If you have access to an online version of the article, the 'find' function can be of particular use.

You can input the key terms/phrases and the 'find' function will skim the whole article for you. However, you should be careful with this method as it is only as good as your search terms. Therefore it can be useful to search for the same idea with a variety of different search terms and try to be aware of where the article/book was written; for example, 'Early Years Foundation Stage' (EYFS) may be referred to as 'Kindergarten', or 'primary school' as 'elementary school'.

SCANNING

Scanning on the other hand is allowing your eyes to track across the page or sentence, aiming for a basic understanding, but not a deep interrogation. It may be that you use skimming to locate possible sections, and then scanning to confirm that these are the 'important' sections, and thus you highlight these sections to come back to when ready. Do be aware that while having an e-copy is useful for skimming, it can actually be more difficult to scan read from a computer screen. It can be useful when you are scanning reading to populate tables with the basic information of each chapter or article. This means that when you come back to access these in future for intensive reading you can access the table and quickly see what is relevant. A suggested format is shown in Table 2.1.

Table 2.1   Template for scanning reading

Article name	Date published	Research aims	Sample size	Limitations

If you do decide to use the example shown in Table 2.1, this can be a good mechanism for sharing journal articles between you and your peers because not all journals will be relevant to you. If you all share two or three journals between yourselves you can collectively work your way through the key texts in that particular area quite quickly. As with all group work, this approach is only as good as your 'weakest' member, but the fact that you all stand to gain from this approach can be quite motivational for all students.

INTENSIVE

Intensive reading requires time and space to be able to interrogate the text that you are reading. It is most likely that intensive reading will be reading on the same topic or perhaps by the same author and, in this way, it lacks the depth and breadth which extensive reading can offer. However, what it does provide is a narrow lens focus that can be a useful view for 'getting to grips with a topic'. It can be very helpful to adopt self-questioning strategies, considering what you have read and what it means at the end of each section. This will hopefully prevent you from reading an entire chapter or article and wondering what you have just read. It can be useful when reading to have a packet of post-it notes with you while you are reading and to try to summarise the key ideas or conclusion on to these post-it notes. You may find as you continue reading that you might want to rephrase or readjust some of the terms that you have used initially in light of new readings. However, it is hoped that eventually, after completing your reading, you start to see the same ideas/conclusions emerging and you do not need to write any more post-it notes. This means that you now know it is time to stop reading and start writing.

EXTENSIVE

As intensive reading is a narrow lens focus, extensive reading is the wider lens. This type of reading is prolonged and helps you to understand how the ideas that you might have read about in your more focused intensive reading are connected to each other and to other topics. This type of reading can be useful in helping you to become a professional teacher as your ideas do not exist in silos but rather they are synergetic. To achieve extensive reading it is important that there is an element of enjoyment from the reading, which will sustain the reading process over time. It is very much hoped that this text helps to develop your extensive reading.

PLACEMENT

GETTING UP AND RUNNING: FOCUS ON TEACHER STANDARD 7

No teaching and learning can take place until the behaviour management of a class is appropriate to pupils' needs. Therefore, this section will start with a focus on behaviour management considering Teacher Standard 7 (DfE, 2011). However, before considering this, let us first look at the ground-work and practical steps you can take regarding behaviour management when starting a placement.

The first place you should start when considering behaviour management in any placement setting is the behaviour policy of that particular school. Many of these policies share similar ideas and language; however, each will be unique to that particular school setting and the children who attend. For example, some schools use bells and whistles while others simply use non-verbal signs when they require pupils' attention. Some schools have a visible behaviour chart with pupils' names on it, while others keep individual rewards and sanctions private. A whole-school approach is important. In the most successful schools, all staff have a clear understanding of what is, and is not, expected from the children within the school and are empowered to act accordingly. Being able to 'fit in' with your school's behaviour policy from day one not only provides continuity and sets expectations for the children, it also helps you to be viewed as a teacher from the start of your placement, as the pupils, across the school, are familiar with the rewards and consequences.

The second consideration is what happens within the classroom(s) where you spend your time. All the classes will follow the school behaviour policy but the ways in which this is implemented might be slightly different in each class. For example, in some classes, there might be a focus on trying to encourage group work across the class and so the class may receive rewards when positive behaviour occurs as a team. In other classes, individual strategies might be employed. It is particularly important that you speak to the teacher about any personalised needs and strategies required for individual children, perhaps as a result of a special educational need or disability. It would be useful to know if any of the children in the class have an individual behaviour plan (IBP), an individual education plan (IEP) or an individual health care plan (IHCP). Some schools do not share the actual plans themselves with trainee teachers; if this is the case, it is useful for you to ask what strategies/support it recommends for which types of situations. Even if none of the children in your class have individual plans, it is also worth having a conversation with the teacher about seating plans and if there are any children who should not perhaps sit together or who may benefit from being closer to the board. It may seem that there is a lot of groundwork to be done, in the form of reading and having discussions, but it is important that this be conducted, ideally before you start teaching. It is important because it helps to keep the children you are teaching safe and secure as well as looking after you, and your mental health. It can be very dispiriting to learn that you have done something 'wrong' after you have done it. Therefore, as far as possible it would be best to learn as much in advance as possible. That does not mean that you will not make mistakes, nor that you should not, but you will make fewer mistakes.

TEACHER STANDARD 7

Let us turn our attention now to the Teacher Standard 7 (DfE, 2011), which focuses on behaviour management, and unpick the statement a little more. It reads, 'Manage behaviour effectively to ensure a good and safe learning environment' (DfE, 2011). This is key. You are not simply managing behaviour for quiet children or children who carry out instructions the first time (although each of these examples is appropriate based in the holistic scope of the Teacher Standard 7). No, the focus is creating an environment where learning can not only take place but also flourish.

Furthermore, it should also be noted that you are trying to create an environment where you as a teacher can flourish. Poor pupil behaviour is often
cited as one of the reasons why teachers leave the profession (Williams,
2018). At one end of the poor behaviour spectrum is violent and threatening
behaviour from children, which while rare is of course very upsetting and
should not be tolerated. However, at the other end of the spectrum and
much more common is low-level disruption. This type of poor behaviour
often means that the children engaged in it are off-task, other children in the
class are unable to concentrate and the teacher is slowly 'ground down' over
a period of days, weeks and years. Therefore, it is of paramount importance
that an appropriate teaching and learning environment is created for all.

The first sub-standard of Teacher Standard 7 states, 'have clear rules
and routines for behaviour in classrooms, and take responsibility for
promoting good and courteous behaviour both in classrooms and around
the school, in accordance with the school's behaviour policy', and the next
states, 'have high expectations of behaviour, and establish a framework for
discipline with a range of strategies, using praise, sanctions and rewards
consistently and fairly' (DfE, 2011). These sub-standards are important
because they allow all children to know what behaviour is expected and
what will happen as a result. Some of these consequences may be positive
while others will be negative in the hope that these will decrease the likelihood
of poor behaviour choices. It could be suggested that this sub-standard
leans towards a behaviourist view of learning and so a whistle-stop tour of
behaviourism may be useful before we continue.

Behaviourists were primarily concerned with observable actions. In addition,
a behaviourist view of learning focuses on changes in the amount and/or the
form of these observable actions. In response to stimulus, a 'correct' response
is demonstrated. Behaviourists were not too bothered about what was going
on inside someone's head (e.g. cognitive changes) as long as their behaviour
changed.

Behaviourism takes the view that learning is a result of different experience,
favouring associative learning. Associative learning can be split further
into two forms: classical conditioning and operant conditioning. Perhaps
the most famous of the behaviourists, with his work with/on dogs, is
Pavlov. Pavlov (1902), when working on a separate area of digestion,
noticed that the dogs which he was working with would salivate when
presented with their food. Over time, the dogs began to respond to the
presence of the handler (to open the food) or the noise of the feeding
device prior to actually receiving the food and would salivate without the
food being present, as they had linked these stimuli with food. Pavlov
later retrained the dogs to salivate at the sound of a bell. This is called

classical conditioning. Learning through classical conditioning means that a stimulus is able to create a response, which was originally linked to another stimulus.

Watson and Rayner (1920) took this work further. This is probably best illustrated by Watson and Rayner's controversial experiment (which certainly would not receive ethical approval nowadays) with a baby commonly known as Little Albert. In this experience, a nine-month-old baby (Albert) was introduced to a series of stimulus including a white rat, a rabbit, a monkey, masks and burning newspapers. Initially Albert did not show any fear of these stimuli. However, when he was exposed to them again these items were accompanied by a loud noise, which made the baby cry. Eventually, by paring the white rat and the loud noise, Albert would cry simply at the sight of the white rat. This experiment can be broken down into the steps of classical conditioning:

1   Neutral stimulus: the white rat
2   Unconditioned stimulus: the loud noise
3   Unconditioned response: fear
4   Conditioned stimulus: the white rat
5   Conditioned response: fear.

Skinner (1938) is known for his work with rats, whom he rewarded with food if they exhibited a certain behaviour, meaning that the rats learned to repeat the behaviour. This is known as operant conditioning because the behaviour the rats exhibited was not one that they would naturally exhibit, but instead took place because of learning. Skinner also suggested that negative and positive reinforcement could increase or decrease the likelihood of something happening. For example, consider a pupil in your class who always shouts out the answers and interrupts and distracts the other children; you might give in and take their answer to get them to be quiet. However, because you have positively reinforced (by taking the answer) the misbehaviour (shouting out, not raising a hand), they will probably be more likely to act out again in the future in order to receive another treat.

A behaviourist approach is reliant on external stimuli, which generally stem from you, the teacher. As this approach is only concerned with observable behaviours, as a teacher you cannot be sure if your student has really understood something or if they are just 'performing'. So if we return to the 'have clear rules and routines for behaviour in classrooms, and take responsibility for promoting good and courteous behaviour both in classrooms and around the school, in accordance with the school's behaviour policy'

(DfE, 2011), as a trainee teacher you need to ensure that you are consistent. You need to ensure that all children understand these roles and routines, are supported to follow them and that pupils are rewarded or sanctioned as appropriate. This is because the behaviourist motivation stems from the teacher, and so without you present you may find that your pupils do not exhibit the same behaviour, as there is no internal drive. This leads us quite nicely on to other approaches to learning, which may actually increase pupils' own motivations for learning and desired behaviours.

As behaviourists are concerned with observable changes to behaviour, cognitivists are interested in changes to thinking. Piaget and Vygotsky are two of the key authors in this area. Piaget (1952) proposed that all children have schemas; these are the internal 'thinking maps' that children create, update and change, ever expanding their scope as they grow. A child may have a schema that all cats are black and as they encounter big and small, and fat and thin black cats this 'fits' the schema they already have (assimilation), until they see a ginger cat. Then they may indeed question if the ginger cat is a cat. Once informed it is, they will then adapt their existing schema to take account of this new information (accommodation). When a child's world experiences fit with their schema, they can be said to be in equilibrium. Piaget (1952) also suggested four stages of cognitive development:

- sensorimotor (0–2)
- preoperational (2–7)
- concrete operational (7–11)
- formal operational (11+).

So how does this link back to creating the 'right' climate for learning? Well, Piaget (1958) felt that the processes of assimilation and accommodation were 'active processes' and as such required problem-solving and discovery learning. This is quite different from the controlled, stimulus–reaction link that behaviourists tend to favour. If we take the third sub-standard, which reads 'manage classes effectively, using approaches which are appropriate to pupils' needs in order to involve and motivate them' (DfE, 2011), it would therefore seem appropriate to consider a cognitivist approach. This is because from a behaviourist point of view the motivation is external, it comes from rewards. What can be useful in your teaching is to help children develop an internal, sometimes known as intrinsic, motivation. Interestingly, this can be located not in Teacher Standard 7 but in Teacher Standard 2, 'encourage pupils to take a responsible and conscientious attitude to their own work and study' (DfE, 2011), Teacher Standard 4, 'promote a love of learning and children's intellectual curiosity' (DfE, 2011), and Teacher Standard 3, 'foster ... pupils' interest in the subject, ... promote the value of scholarship' (DfE, 2011).

The final sub-standard states, 'maintain good relationships with pupils, exercise appropriate authority, and act decisively when necessary' (DfE, 2011). One could suggest that this follows a humanist perspective. The humanist movement is based on the work of Maslow (1943, 1954) (in particular his Hierarchy of Needs) and Rodgers and has since been built upon by Montessori and Claremont (1969). This approach favours seeing the child as a 'whole' and looking to develop self-esteem, enabling children to manage their own emotions and set realistic objectives. This approach also encourages learning with/through peers as well as through the teacher. Through maintaining good relationships, with appropriate boundaries, as a teacher you will be able to understand each child in your class better. This means that you will be able to personalise the learning experience to best fit each child.

In reality, none of these approaches exists in isolation and so it can sometimes be misleading to present them as such. However, it is hoped that by approaching Teacher Standard 7 in this way you can start to see the multifaceted nature of the Teachers' Standards, and how they can interweave different approaches.

MENTAL HEALTH AND WELLBEING

TO DO:
WHY
Be a teacher

If you are reading this book before you start your course, make a note on a post-it about how you feel. Consider all of your hopes, thoughts and feelings. What you are worried about and how do you plan to address these worries? However, most importantly write why you want to be a teacher. The more detail the better. This is because at the start of a teacher training course, it is the happiest you will feel until you graduate. This is not to say that there will not be amazing moments, or fantastic days; of course there will. Nevertheless, learning to teach is very different from other courses that you may have undertaken previously or that friends are studying for at the moment. This is because the professional standards, to which you are accountable from day one, are the same for trainees as for more experienced teachers.

UNCONSCIOUS INCOMPETENCE

In my experience, all student teachers tend to move through the same stages over the course of their training from unconscious incompetence through to unconscious competence (Broadwell, 1969). Almost everyone at the start of the year tends to literally shimmer and shine from their lecture hall seats, and why shouldn't they? They have just been accepted into a competitive course for one of the most rewarding jobs you can have. They are ready to inspire learners. Make a difference. Campaign for social justice. However, it is at this point most student teachers have no idea what they do not know. Yes, of course they are not completely ignorant; most teachers are aware of subjects or concepts, which they feel they will need to 'brush up' on. However, the true enormity of what a student teacher needs to know has not yet revealed itself. They are still unconsciously incompetent.

CONSCIOUS INCOMPETENCE

As you start in school, it is what could be described as a 'slow burn'. You undertake lots of observations and some group work and of course little aspects that you are not familiar with start to emerge, you may even complete several subject knowledge audits, which again start to highlight the gaps in your knowledge. As you attend lectures and your assignments are presented to you, these might also start to draw your attention to what you do not know. Moreover, somewhere between the start of the course and teaching your first lessons it starts to dawn on you just what you do not know. Unfortunately, this is not a single completed action, which happens; this is a collection of experiences, which form over a series of weeks at the start of your first placement. However, as soul destroying as you may find this process, having now read about it here should give you a sense of achievement because you have just transitioned from being unconsciously incompetent to consciously incompetent. This is the first step in being able to address the gaps that you might have. In addition, simply knowing that this is perfectly normal can help. Most trainee teachers complete some form of work experience before embarking on their chosen career, and this is helpful; however, I am not sure it can ever really prepare you for the enormity of the role that you will start to assume over time. Teaching as a profession is further complicated by the fact that as everyone has been to school, it can be misleading to feel that teaching is 'understood' by all. Great teaching happens quite often before the teacher steps into the classroom and what is observable is really the last segment of this complicated process. Great teaching starts with the research or the evidence, is supported by considering how best to personalise this learning through bespoke delivery, which matches the students in the class, and then is reflected upon and changes are made for the future. This becomes clear to the trainee teacher when they start to teach, as they do not yet have that back catalogue of experience and knowledge from which to draw. However, good relationships with your mentor in school are invaluable here as they can really support you and develop you until you are ready to 'go solo'.

Importance of good relationship with your → mentor

When you are consciously incompetent, there are several reactions you may have: face up and take action, head down and ignore, head bobble and mind wobble. Let us have a look at the advantages and disadvantages of each one of these as an approach.

FACE UP AND TAKE ACTION

Being able to acknowledge your own points for development, what you know and don't know, is a key skill to develop as a trainee teacher and is actually part of Teacher Standard 8, 'develop effective professional relationships with colleagues, knowing how and when to draw on advice and specialist support; take responsibility for improving teaching through appropriate professional development, responding to advice and feedback from colleagues' (DfE, 2011). The trainees who make the most progress over their training are not those who have the most experience, nor those who begin teaching well; in fact, they are those trainees who seek out support when needed, listen and consider the feedback openly, and then take action when needed. It can be difficult sometimes to hear feedback when you feel that you have invested much time and effort in teaching a lesson and it did not go as well as planned. However, as teaching is a performance sport (e.g. you cannot go away and practise this in private), this is unfortunately how you learn. That said, your mentor is not looking for you to be perfect; far from it, they can remember training too. Instead, what they are looking for is your ability to look at the learning that has taken place in your classroom because of your teaching. If the pupils have been learning, you need to consider why; and if they have not learned what you would have liked them to have, then again you need to consider why. You are not a robot and you will not always 'get it right'. Nevertheless, at the end of the day the question that you have to ask yourself is: did you do the best today that you could do, with the resources you had available (time/illness/other commitments)? And if the answer is yes, then you've done enough. If the answer is no, you certainly shouldn't beat yourself up but you should consider how you might like to ensure that this doesn't happen again.

HEAD DOWN AND IGNORE

Some trainee teachers are very uncomfortable revealing what they do not know in their school. This can place them in a precarious position where they may feel compelled to pretend that everything is OK, when in fact they are struggling. In my experience, this type of reaction comes from how confident the trainee teacher is and how comfortable they are in what could be considered a vulnerable position. If a trainee teacher is unable to ask for help or feels that they have to wear a 'mask' in school, this pressure tends to build until later in the year the student might start to 'crack' or 'explode'. Sometimes, students taking this approach do not even 'admit to themselves' how they are truly feeling and what they do not know, and these students really struggle to improve. It would be my advice, if possible, to try to speak about how you feel over something that you consider 'low stakes' as early as you can. This way you can start to practise becoming confident in this area. Using your weekly meetings with your mentor can be a useful point to discuss aspects you are not sure about. Eventually, like anything that you practise, you will be better at it, and it is a key skill, which will help you throughout your career.

HEAD BOBBLE, MIND WOBBLE

This approach is somewhere in between the 'face up and take action' and the 'head down and ignore' approaches. In this approach students tend to realise that there might be things that they do not know, feel worried about this, but then become almost 'swamped' by the emotions that they are experiencing. These trainees usually feel that everyone else is 'doing OK', that it is just them struggling, and then the fear that they feel starts to penetrate into other areas of the course. This type of student tends to spiral down into an emotionally difficult place, as they are aware of the areas for development, but are rendered unable to tackle these areas due to the overwhelming negative feelings. In this instance, taking quite a pragmatic approach can be useful. On a piece of paper, write down all of the aspects that are bothering you. You know what these are already, but writing in coherent sentences is different from all of your thoughts being jumbled in your head; by writing them down your thoughts are stream-lined and filtered (we look at this approach more in Chapters 3 and 4). Then look at breaking down each of these 'thoughts' into their competent actions. For example, if paperwork is bothering you, which paperwork? Can you then break down this idea further, so that it contains some actionable verbs? For example:

1   Buy a folder.
2   Buy dividers.
3   File pile of papers from under the bed into each section.
4   Complete missing evaluations
5   Print off missing lesson plans.
6   Include on weekly meeting form to ask mentor for missing lesson observation.

The 'trap' that students often fall into is listing all the 'jobs' but these jobs are actually outcomes. The best example to illustrate this is the task to clean the house. This on its own is not possible to action; you have to break it down into its component parts: wipe the surfaces, take the bins out, hoover the carpet and dust the skirting boards. Each one of these jobs is actionable. Some take longer than others do and some can be fitted into an afternoon. However, by having these listed and being able to tick off each one you start to feel like you have control again and that you are making progress.

CONSCIOUS COMPETENCE

Good news: the next transition is from consciously incompetent to consciously competent. This sneaky transition creeps up while you are not aware of it. Being consciously competent means that you are able to teach and your pupils learn as a result; however, this is not easy. You need to work very hard to ensure that all of your plates are spinning. It is like when you learned to drive a car, and you had to concentrate on checking mirrors, had to look at the gear stick before changing gear and certainly could not listen to the radio at the same time as driving. It is at this point trainees often feel that they are not making progress because it does not feel 'easy'. It is getting 'easier' and actually the level at which you are performing is higher and keeps developing. If when you get to this point you do not think you have made any progress whatsoever, you should cast your mind back to the start of the year when you started to teach your first group or lesson and you will quickly see that simply this is not the case. The trick for this phase is to keep going. Keep putting one step in front of the other and just do not give up or become disheartened. You are doing it! You are being a teacher at this point; it is just a bit of a slog and the chances are that you are just plain old knackered by this point so remember to look after yourself.

UNCONSCIOUS COMPETENCE

Finally, the last transition is from consciously competent to unconsciously competent. This move does not tend to happen across your teaching all in one go. You may find that there are lessons or days or groups where you get what is called 'flow' and other days where it is still quite a struggle. If you are aware of this, you can start to enjoy those days when it does indeed 'flow'. Eventually, most parts of your teaching will move over into the 'flow' side. However, if you change schools or change year groups it is possible that over your teaching career you move between these two states and being aware of this is really helpful in 'future proofing' yourself so you don't ever give yourself a hard time unnecessarily.

It may be useful to print out the graph in Figure 2.1 and have it on your wall at home. It can be useful for a number of reasons:

1   In a handy glance, you can see you will be successful.
2   You can see your entire life cycle as a trainee in one view.
3   If you are finding it hard, and you are in and out of the 'trenches',* you will know it will not last for ever.
4   Your friends and family can also see you will not be grumpy for ever.

* Depending on your course format, after an initial downwards trajectory you may find you have a series of mini ups and downs before finally going on the up and up. However, it is important to remember that overall you will be going up. It is just really slow and really hard.

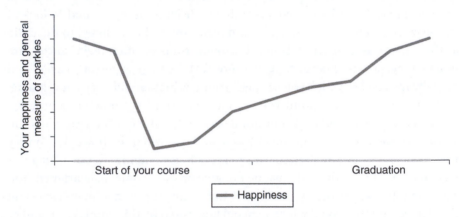

Figure 2.1   Trainee teacher happiness over the entirety of their course

CASE STUDY 2.1   THE YOUNG(ISH) EX-SPORTS COACH

Let us introduce Jamie. Jamie used to be a sports coach before he joined the teaching course. He loves working with children and what's more the children adore Jamie. Jamie had not really considered teaching before becoming a coach, but after completing his sport development degree and seeing all of his friends starting to get jobs Jamie became increasingly worried about employment and thought that teaching might be a natural fit. One of Jamie's friends became a teacher and told Jaime that coaching children in school was really enjoyable. Jamie decided to try this out, and really enjoyed coaching the children, and the kids all really liked Jamie's one session a week in their school.

Jamie did not read many of the policies before starting school because he is confident in his own abilities to 'get the children on side'. Jamie loves getting involved with games at lunch and always helps at the after-school clubs. After all, this approach has worked for Jamie before. Jamie is able to integrate PE across the curriculum in a meaningful way, and sometimes the teachers in his placement school ask for advice. Jamie is also really looking forward to being a student again; it was such a laugh before. However, because Jamie has other social commitments such as playing football three times a week, plus seeing mates and working, he does not always go into lectures or sessions, but he does not really feel like he is missing out. After all it is all up on the VLE (virtual learning environment) so he can just catch up at home. Jamie has got all the necessary paperwork and next weekend, as long as nothing comes up, he just needs to sort it all out and put it in the right places, and maybe just catch up on two weeks of evaluations and some observations. He's not really too sure but has a sheet somewhere that a friend gave him with all the jobs on so he's going to work his way down the form, once he finds it.

Maybe you read the paragraphs above and thought, 'Yup, that's me!' or perhaps it describes someone you know on your course, or it just picks out elements of your personality. In which case consider the suggestions below carefully. Maybe none of the above seems familiar, but it might be that in about five years after qualifying, when you are the mentor, you might meet 'this student'. It is then better to try to understand their strengths and their areas for development before you encounter them in your classroom.

Let us consider the following questions: What are Jamie's strengths and how can these be maximised on placement? What are Jamie's areas for development? Why do you think he has these points for development?

Jamie's strengths are that he is well received by both pupils and teachers alike. He is an affable character who is willing to 'pitch in' when required and is always a pleasure to have around. Jamie has a skill set already developed from coaching children and a desire to work with children. Jamie also has good subject knowledge in the area of PE and as such can work with other teachers to upskill these teachers. This means that as well as learning from more experienced professionals Jamie is also able to offer something back to his placement school. This is important in developing a sense of identity and confidence on placement.

(Continued)

Sometimes you may feel that you are always asking questions and seeking support. However, if you have a key strength then you can offer to lead a club or support planning in this area and, depending on the subject (e.g. foreign languages, music and PE most commonly), you may find that you are one of a small group.

Jamie's possible weaknesses are that he has failed to realise the distinction between studying on a course and participating on a professional degree course such as teaching. As a result, Jamie has not updated his identity to match the 'job' that he is now doing. This means that by not reading policies, attending university sessions or completing paperwork he is not really sure of what he should be doing and when. Jamie will be able to 'struggle' through for a while, but eventually action will have to be taken if he wishes to have a successful outcome.

It is likely that Jamie may struggle with how to be organised, and that previous methods do not work on such a busy course as there are simply too many plates to spin. Jamie should read Chapters 3 and 5 with care to better understand how to get the most out of sessions. Jamie should also start with a wall planner (key dates), programme his phone with reminders two weeks before key dates, have a diary and a 'things to do today' list. Jamie should actively seek out a Busy Working Parent to make friends with (see Chapter 6) and to learn time-management skills.

CHAPTER SUMMARY

- Read; and then read some more. More importantly read before attempting to write.
- Get to know your children and know them well. Generic behaviour approaches will work with generic children. Unfortunately, you won't have any of these in your class.
- Have high expectations of behaviour from the start and do not compromise.
- Focus on the positives in your classroom. Use verbal praise to identify and name the behaviour you would like to see more of.
- Expect not to know things about teaching and how to be a teacher. Things take time. Be kind to yourself.

FURTHER READING

Buckler, S. and Castle, P. (2018) *Psychology for Teachers*, 2nd edition. London: Sage.

This book is a great read for anyone interested in the different approaches to education (behaviourist, humanist, psychodynamic, cognitive, etc.). In addition, the text provides a comprehensive overview of how you can empower your learners through motivation and developing psychological skills.

Cremin, T. and Burnett, C. (eds) (2018) *Learning to Teach in the Primary School*, 4th edition (Learning to Teach in the Primary School Series). London: Routledge.

There are great sections in this book for a whole host of topics, but the section on behaviour is particularly good. It lifts the concept of behaviour from simply being about rewards and sanctions and elevates it to being about holistic teaching.

Headspace app: www.headspace.com/headspace-meditation-app (accessed 4 September 2019).

This is a free app (although there are paid content aspects too), which provides guided meditations. Please do not expect to simply listen once and feel relaxed. You will need to practise these and give it a little time. However, once you have got the hang of it, you can simply take a 'pause' in your day for two minutes by listening to it.

3

UNIVERSITY SUPPORT, CLASSROOM PLANNING AND THE POWER OF REFLECTION

This
CHAPTER
EXPLORES:

- why it is important to go to university and the types of support it can give you
- the importance of being clear on planning your pupils' learning objectives
- how to do a mind and body scan to find out how you feel.

ACADEMIC

IS THERE ANY POINT GOING TO UNIVERSITY?

As the workload throughout a teacher training course increases rapidly, so does the decline in student attendance at university sessions. Students rarely miss placement, but depending on prior experiences may feel that it is reasonable to skip university sessions to 'catch up' on work. In the long run this strategy does not actually save time or help the student to complete what they have to because actually these students can end up less informed and missing deadlines. Furthermore, it can be detrimental to the long-term teaching career of such a student as they only have a surface understanding of areas. A feeling of isolation, of not being part of the cohort, can start to creep in, leading to a vicious cycle of not wanting to go into sessions as these students experience feelings of 'not belonging' and so they miss classes, and on and on. Therefore, this section will explore what universities can offer through their teacher training courses. Basically, why should you attend? However, the first topic to be considered is the difference between your academic work and your recommendation for QTS, because it is not always clear for students what each aspect is related to.

When undertaking a teacher education course, unless it is a QTS-only route there will usually be an academic component to your course. For example, if you are undertaking an undergraduate course, your modules from Levels 5 and 6 will contribute towards your degree classification (academic component). However, to be able to gain recommendation for qualified teacher status you must also pass your placements through evidencing the Teachers' Standards.

This means that you can demonstrate that you have met the Teachers' Standards in all of the key stages as per your degree. If you are undertaking a PGCE (Postgraduate Certificate in Education), it is your modules from Level 7 that will provide you with the academic credits, and then the placement which will gain you recommendation for QTS. Most institutions also embed the QTS part into one of the core modules, meaning that the placement and the academic part need to be passed together. It is entirely possible to do either one of these 'parts' on their own, and gain either an academic qualification in education without the recommendation for QTS, or to just gain QTS (provided you pass the module the QTS sits in). There are of course jobs in schools which advertise for non-qualified teachers, so the question is: why put yourself through a teacher education course? This is a good question. Now, before you all rush off to withdraw yourselves from your current course, this topic needs closer inspection as there are many reasons why you should embark on a teacher education course, which we will now consider.

RESEARCH INFORMED

University teacher education courses are research informed and. as such, they provide entry for new teachers into the world of educational research. In fact, most university courses are mandated to include a research module on postgraduate courses and elements of research practice in their under-graduate programmes. This ensures a level of criticality within both the curriculum and for the teachers undertaking the course. Research skills are important for teachers entering the profession. They enable teachers to reflect on their own practice and seek answers to real life issues in their class-rooms. By participating in research skill development at university, trainee teachers ensure that they will develop their own research toolkit from which to draw upon in the future.

The lecturers delivering specific modules will be specialists in their chosen area, quite often conducting their own research within this area, which they can draw upon and share. It should be noted here, quite clearly, that research is not something which belongs exclusively to universities/lecturers, far from it. Many teachers are involved in research on a daily basis. However, there is a numbers game to consider. Most universities are able to draw upon specialist support in a variety of areas simply due to size. The business of schools is to educate its pupils, and while mentoring and coaching trainee teachers is an element of this, it is an additional factor. Some teachers receive remission hours for this role, while others do not. Many teachers have such busy workloads that it can be difficult for them to find the time to share research and evidence with their student teachers. Trainee teachers through attending university courses are able 'to learn from university lecturers who are steeped in, and practised at, navigating their way through these [educational] debates, [which] cannot be underestimated' (Gewirtz, 2013: 12). This means that a multiplicity of approaches is more easily presented within the university context rather than perhaps only a particular school's or specific chain of schools' approach. There is nothing wrong with a specific approach, but you may find as a teacher if you move to a different school or area that the specific 'school brand' of teaching and learning that you studied simply does not work in another setting or demographic. It can be useful to learn about a plethora of approaches and ideas, even if they do not seem initially relevant to your preferred way of teaching. For example, each year I used to liaison tutor a group of students who went on a placement in the Canary Islands (sadly, that route into teaching has now closed). The pupils in the school where my students were on placement did not wear uniforms and all learned from the same textbook as there was no differentiation. It was always interesting to observe the trainee teachers' reactions to this teaching and learning context, as there were some real contrasts in approaches. Initially, the trainee teachers would reject the approach as a whole, but over the course of the placement, they would reposition their own views and ideologies, and by the end of the placement they had a new, internationally informed perspective. This is not to say that you need to go abroad to gain a new perspective, questioning alternative approaches works too, although it could be recommended if you get the chance.

SPACE FOR REFLECTION

Schools are very busy places. That is not to say that university is not busy, in fact on a teacher education course, you are among the students with the higher percentage of contact hours. However, what is built into your course as well as your assignments is time for reflection: to stop and to consider what you saw or did and why this might have occurred as well as other approaches that you could have or should have taken. Many courses also introduce their students to models of reflection including 'critical incident analysis' (Tripp, 1993) (note: this is not nearly as scary as it sounds). If you are in school 100 per cent of the time, the chances are that even weekly meetings and lunchtimes are interrupted and you simply would not get the chance to stop and consider your practice.

When on placement, your targets and focus tend to be on a lesson-to-lesson basis and then eventually on units of work. The space to consider the larger educational issues is very difficult to find in busy schools. In addition it can be difficult for the trainee teacher to question the 'status quo', which they might have noticed while working in school. However, by talking, chatting and discussing with peers and your tutor you are able to develop your own views about education, and clarify and redefine your own views, which sometimes trainee teachers were not fully aware of until called to speak aloud.

TRAINEE TEACHER COMMUNITY

When embarking on a teaching course you already have a ready-made group of peers who are all experiencing the same challenges and opportunities as you as you all navigate your way through the learning. This is certainly not to say that there is no online community for teaching, of course there is, but sometimes trainee teachers' voices can get a little lost. Furthermore, when you are training there can be a lack of confidence in questioning ideas or revealing a concern that you have, which you certainly would not feel comfortable doing in a public space. However, when chatting informally with other students on your course you can begin to understand a wide array of perspectives about teaching and learning. Quite frankly, no one will understand your teacher development journey quite like someone else on your course. Not all of them will be to your liking, maybe some are (delete as applicable) idiots/annoying/immature/barking mad, but you know what? Whether or not you like your fellow students, they are your people, and you are all in it together. It is a difficult course to complete, so try not to isolate yourself. Much better to be accompanied and working hard than isolated and working hard. You never know, over time some of them will work their way into your heart.

AVAILABILITY OF WIDER UNIVERSITY SERVICES (E.G. COUNSELLING, CAREERS SERVICE, LIBRARY AND GYM)

When you join a teacher education programme you are also joining a university and this brings with it a variety of benefits. Perhaps the first and most important benefit is the student discount. With new suppliers recently providing an array of discounts housed in the same space (e.g. unidays) getting cashback and discounted shopping has become easier. There are also more 'serious' benefits. One of the most important is the health and wellbeing services that universities offer to their students. This suite of services tends to include occupational health. Occupational health is concerned with ensuring that the student and staff body are well and supported at work/study. This department also has a remit for supporting individuals with long-term health conditions/disabilities and ensuring that they can achieve their potential. You will most likely be sent a questionnaire to complete before commencing your course and should your university need to ask for further information they will invite you in to have a discussion.

Many universities also offer a selection of wellbeing services. The offer is different from institution to institution; however, most commonly there are usually different sessions, which look at common issues facing students such as anxiety or body image. Sometimes these can be difficult for a trainee teacher to gain access to, as you are either on placement or in university for whole days. If there is a session that you feel would benefit you, it is always worth speaking to your mentor or your lecturer to see if you could leave a university session a little earlier to attend. If you are on placement, you could always see if you could negotiate to have your PPA at this time and then complete your planning at home later instead. It is important that you try to address any issues that you might be facing earlier rather than later when they are 'bigger'. While you may not want to miss part of a university session or leave a placement earlier, this can be preferable to not addressing a situation and eventually having to take more time off later on in the year.

In addition to group sessions, which tend to focus on common issues that students face, universities are also increasingly offering online support, usually in the form of Silver Cloud or the Big White Wall. Silver Cloud is based on cognitive behavioural therapy techniques and is available 24/7 online. This is important because it allows you to access support when you need it rather than during 'office hours'. This support service operates through 'theme', e.g. anxiety, stress, self-image, and allows you to navigate your own pathway through the modules, dipping in and out, as you choose. Simply search for this on your university's webpages and sign up. If your university does not offer Silver Cloud the chances are that it offers instead the Big White Wall. The Big White Wall is a safe space to talk about mental health online. There are a number of ways in which you can engage with this service such as peer and professional support and creative self-expression. The online courses which it provides are evidence-based and include managing stress and anxiety as well as more general topics such as healthy eating and smoking cessation. The service is moderated by trained counsellors who are online at all times and can provide further support if required. Occasionally, the Big White Wall also provides face-to-face therapy online, using its own experienced therapists or with NHS clinicians. These two services can be useful for trainee teachers, as you do not need to negotiate time out of your busy schedules to be able to access them.

Universities also offer their students counselling services to discuss issues of a personal or emotional nature. These sessions are with a trained counsellor on a one-to-one confidential basis. Recently, universities have been experiencing an increase in demand for counselling services. One of the reasons for this is that students often use this as the first port of call rather than the last in a series of supports, which are available (see mental health section in Chapter 4 for self-care ideas). However, if you are experiencing mental health concerns of a serious nature, particularly if are concerned you may injure yourself or *if you are feeling like you want to die, it is important to tell someone*. Do not wait to go through your university services. You can contact instead the Samaritans: 116 123 or email jo@samaritans.org. In a non-emergency situation you can contact your GP or call 111. However, if you have seriously harmed yourself, or you are worried about a friend who has seriously harmed themselves, e.g. a drug overdose, you must call 999 or go to A&E straight away.

Universities also have good careers services, which you can access to find summer jobs or even to gain support with the writing of CVs and applications for jobs. Many teacher education courses, in addition to the central university service, will also provide you with support in applying for your first position, including mock interviews with headteachers, sessions with supply agencies, and inviting NQTs and RQTs to come in and speak to you about their first year in employment. Of course, schools and chains of schools provide advice in this area too, but again, due to the size of the institution, the careers service is a dedicated department specifically for helping you in this area. This means availability, time and space are usually more accessible than if you were to ask a busy class teacher. However, these options are not mutually exclusive and, as such, you should engage with all help that is available.

Your university library may not be the most exciting student space on campus. However, access to a university's library facilities and amazing librarians is a real gift, which should not be underestimated (see Chapter 6 for 'Online offerings').

In conclusion, yes, there will be days when you do not feel like attending university and you may feel that you have more to gain by staying at home and 'catching up'. However, this is a very short-term strategy, which in the long term will not make you a better teacher. It actually may mean that you miss more and fall even more behind (see Chapter 5 for 'Making seminars and small groups work for you'), so start to feel worse as you become socially and academically isolated. Furthermore, you have probably paid a significant amount of money in fees to have access to all of these support mechanisms, so use them.

PLACEMENT

PLANNING

Planning is a key focus of any student teacher's placement experience. However, it is a tortuous skill to learn. Unfortunately, the only way to get better at this is to practise. In Chapter 2 we considered how to 'get up and running' using Teacher Standard 7 as a focus. In this section, we are going to consider how careful planning, preparation and assessment can further enhance your approach to behaviour management in your classroom. This is because through careful differentiated planning, each child's needs can be catered for, enabling them to access interesting, motivational work. As a result, most children are focused on their learning. In Chapter 2 we focused solely on Teacher Standard 7, but it would be worth noting that behaviour management actually intertwines with all of the standards. Perhaps one of the clearest ways to see this is by the terms 'preventative', 'reorientation' and 'reactive' approaches to behaviour management that Cremin and Arthur (2014) use. They break down behaviour management into these three categories, with the aim of using this as a sort of traffic light system. The main idea is that by planning interesting lessons, which are at the right 'pitch' and differentiate appropriately, and by giving assessment feedback, most children remain in the green/preventative area.

This section on planning aims to provide a slightly different slant from other texts that you may have already read about planning. This is not designed to be a systematic guide nor does it aim to provide a deep insight

into planning. It is, however, designed to be an accessible read, to contextualise the process and purpose of planning. Over the years, it has been noticed
that planning is often seen as 'just another job' – that trainee teachers may
rush through to get to the 'enjoyable stuff' such as making resources or teaching. As such, trainees may fail to understand that it is the planning which is
the most important tool you have in the classroom for meeting all the
Teachers' Standards. After all, it is your planning which identifies where you
show that you have set 'high expectations which inspire, motivate and challenge pupils' as seen in Teacher Standard 1 (DfE, 2011), or how you intend to
'promote good progress and outcomes by pupils' as seen in Teacher Standard
2, while of course, demonstrating 'good subject and curriculum knowledge'
(DfE, 2011). We could easily go on to consider the remainder of the Teachers'
Standards, but you get the idea.

HOW TO PLAN

So where do you start? When starting to plan a lesson or a series of lessons you should firstly try to understand what the pupils have previously
been learning and how successful this has been for each child/group. This is
because lessons (unlike lesson plans) do not exist in isolation. Whether you
are in placement teaching all week, or you are only there one day a week,
the teaching and learning is continuous, with or without you. Therefore,
prior learning is where you need to start. You can learn about this by either
accessing prior assessment data or/and having a conversation with the previous teacher. If you do not understand what the data means, you need to
schedule this issue into your next weekly meeting to discuss.

Once you know what your pupils have learned, or what they might need
to revisit first, your next step is to define clearly what you want them to have
learned after your lesson/series of lessons. In very basic terms, what will
your pupils have learned at the end of an hour with you that they couldn't do
before? What is your value added? Now, here comes the tricky bit. Do you
remember in Chapter 2 when we considered the behaviourists? They were
only concerned with observable behaviour, e.g. things that they could see
and things that they could measure. And do you remember at the end of that
section, it was recommended that you do further reading about other
approaches to teaching (cognitivist, constructivist, humanist, etc.) and then
you combine these as appropriate to the needs of your class? Well, that is not
what is being recommended here. What is being recommended is that as you
embark on your teaching career, you frame your learning objectives in what
could be described as a behaviourist approach, using clear measurable verbs.

When you become more proficient and experienced as a teacher, then you can plan learning objectives in whichever way you choose. But having seen trainees struggling with planning over the years, it is usually related to not having clear learning objectives in the first place. Framing objectives in behaviourist language helps to provide clarity around the learning for both you and the children. Clear, measurable verbs are very much your friends in the first instance.

What are clear measurable verbs? These types of verbs allow you to see that learning has taken place. For example, clear learning objectives might include:

- to be able to verbally list five capital cities
- to be able to orally predict what happens next in the story
- to be able to compose music to accompany a specific 'feeling' from art.

Learning objectives should originate from the National Curriculum; more specifically from the subject and year group/key stage that you intent to teach. However, please note that the National Curriculum covers the knowledge/skills that pupils will need to know by the end of that year/key stage and as such should be broken up into incremental steps, which over the year will deliver these overall outcomes. Being able to do this is quite difficult for a trainee teacher, as you have no previous experience of what this year-long journey might actually look like in practice. This is why is it important to work with your class teacher so that you understand what outcomes you are planning for. It may be that your teacher starts you off by giving you the learning objectives from which to plan the lessons.

The opposite of clear measurable learning objectives are what could be referred to as 'fuzzy verbs'. Examples of 'fuzzy verbs' might include:

- to know some capital cities
- to think about the story
- to appreciate music.

If you compare the two learning objectives lists you'll be able to see that the first set are very specific. It is clear that you would like the pupils to be able to verbally list five capital cities, whereas in the second list it is unclear how many capital cities you wish the pupils to know and how they will demonstrate this learning. This may seem pedantic and you might be wondering why this is important; after all, as long as they learn something in the lesson that's the main thing, isn't it? Well, it is and it is not. By having clear, measurable objectives you are then able to assess the learning that has taken place, making sure that there are no gaps in learning. If you are not clear about who has learned what today, then when reviewing planning for tomorrow it will not be clear which pupils should move on and which should revisit the concept again. This is Teacher Standard 6 in action: 'Make accurate and productive use of assessment' (DfE, 2011).

It can be tempting to want to plan based on a resource that you have seen or been recommended, which you are very excited about. However, if you try to plan a lesson around a resource you will find that you may spend a very long time on your planning. This is because you are effectively starting in the middle and trying to reverse engineer the lesson back to an objective, which could really be anything. If you develop good lesson planning habits (e.g. start with behaviourist, clear, measurable objectives), while more boring than using resources as a lesson stimulus, you will find that your planning takes less time than if you did this the other way around.

When planning lesson objectives it is worth considering the cognitive level of what you are asking the pupils do undertake. For example, are you asking them to recall facts or copy from the board (knowledge) or are you asking them to describe or locate (comprehension)? Maybe you are asking them to solve or illustrate a problem (application), maybe comparing and contrasting (analysis), creating or designing (synthesis), evaluating or appraising (evaluation). These levels come from a piece of work by Bloom (1956) and are often referred to as Bloom's taxonomy. The idea of Bloom's taxonomy is to classify learning objectives into levels of challenge. Naturally, within a lesson or across a series of lessons it would be expected that the challenge in cognition provided increases. How would this look over a series of lessons? For example, maybe in your first lesson the pupils are learning the 'facts'. This is 'normal' as students have to have a basic level of knowledge about a topic/concept to be able to then go on to develop what they do with it later. In lesson 2, the pupils could start to describe these ideas themselves. In the next lesson, at the beginning your pupils may need to learn a few more things about what you are studying to be able to create a poster to illustrate the problem to an intended audience. Following on from this, pupils may look at comparing and contrasting two different viewpoints about the same topic and critically evaluate what they have read, or they might propose or design a new way of doing what you have been studying.

To recap so far, when planning you should have considered prior learning, and then set some very clear learning objectives for your lesson or series of lessons, which ensure progression within/across the learning. The next consideration is how you will assess the learning, within the lesson (formative) and at the end of the lesson (summative).

Try to think of the formative assessment as the gear stick for your lessons, if you formatively assess the pupils and they are all on track and understand, you may not need to deliver all of your planned lesson. You could instead set them off to work independently. However, if you check in with the pupils and they are struggling or you start to notice similar errors across the room, then you need to either slow down, reteach or stop and have a mini-plenary to readdress the common misconceptions. Formative assessment is most often in the form of questioning/eliciting information from the pupils in a variety of formats. The format is not necessarily important although each has a particular strength or drawback; for example, '1, 2, 3, show me' on whiteboards means all pupils have to be ready to show you their workings at the same time and are unable to copy, while a lollypop stick approach means that only one child is chosen at a time.

The important point to remember about formative assessment is to not ask a question if you are not prepared to 'do something' about the answer. The questions are not there to make your lesson plan look nice; they are there to adjust the speed of your lesson. And really, you are trying to find the edge of learning, the children who do not understand what you have been teaching. This then allows you do something about it, within the lesson.

Summative assessment is reasonably straightforward, as long as you have started with very clear lesson objectives. If you have clear lesson objectives then you will be able to easily identify what it is that children should be able to do by the end of the lesson/series of lessons. Dylan Wiliam (see Wiliam and Black) said once at a conference, and I paraphrase: 'If you take home 30 books to mark, and you have to write the same thing in all 30 books as they have all made the same mistake, then this is your "punishment" for not having formatively assessed during the lesson.' This could not be truer. When you assess your summative work at the end of the lesson/series of lessons there really should not be any surprises. When considering your assessment of the children's learning consider if you are assessing shallow or deep learning (TSC, 2016: 15)

Another aspect of planning that trainee teachers may struggle with is how to go about planning their own role in the classroom. I often read lesson plans that state, 'the children will ...' repeatedly across the lesson plan with absolutely no mention of what the teacher will do. Simply put, if the children could do X, Y and Z without any input from you, then why are you there? As a teacher, you will be the single most expensive resource in any classroom, so you have to think about why you are there. What will you add or do that would be worth paying you a wage in future? For example, will you model the task for the children, will you demonstrate it or provide children with resources and elicit information through questioning? Again, Bloom's taxonomy can help you to consider your role in the classroom very clearly. Be wary of 'fuzzy teaching verbs'. Most common offenders include 'to introduce'. If you think about it, what would you actual do to achieve this? Of course, you could introduce through showing, or telling or verbally explaining but to introduce on its own is a misdirection. Again, another common one is 'to recap'. Consider instead how you will achieve this, what exactly you will do. Most of the time when you find yourself using these 'fuzzy verbs' then you actually mean that you will simply verbally explain/talk to the children. This is fine if you really consider this to be the best way to teach your class, but you may find that, given a little more detailed consideration about your specific role, there are actually more sophisticated ways of 'recapping' than simple verbal explanations. By considering these aspects in detail, then your teaching is likely to improve as you have more sophisticated plans to support all children in your class through really considered presentation. If you would like further guidance on the types of teaching approaches you could include, see the placement section in Chapter 4.

Subject knowledge and subject pedagogy is important. However, you will not come as the 'complete package' when you start teaching. Nevertheless, you do need to know what you do not know. Then it is just the matter of taking steps to remedy your development areas. Do not make assumptions or think that you know something just because you learned it in a particular way when you were at school. It is always prudent to take the time to research or seek guidance from your mentor during a placement. Through carefully researching a topic, it will also alert you to possible misconceptions that the pupils are making. Remember, through your formative assessment you can really start to understand not only what pupils are doing, but also how they are doing it. Pupils can have the right answers for the wrong reasons, and the wrong answers as a result of a minor mistake in a multi-step problem or process. Asking your pupils why they think what they think or have produced what they have created is enlightening. Do be prepared for some of the most bonkers explanations you have ever heard – it is truly illuminating to hear pupils explain their thinking, while giving you the chance to model thinking for them. If you are interested in this (and you should be because studies show that the language of metacognition can really impact on learners' progress – see Technical Appendix, EEF Teaching and Learning Toolkit Strand 'Metacognition and Self Regulation') then the best place to start for further information would be the EEF Teaching and Learning Toolkit.

The final consideration when planning is how you intend to differentiate for your learners. Differentiation can be described as ensuring that the work you are asking your pupils to complete or participate in provides the right level of challenge. This is important because work that is too easy or too hard could result in learners simply 'switching off'. However, in the words of Goldilocks, you are looking for when the challenge 'is just right'. If you hit the sweet spot, then your pupils will be encouraged and motivated to learn. Setting the 'right' conditions can involve consideration of what it is that you actually want the children to learn and ensuring that the other 'bits' you are asking them to do don't get in the way. The proper term for this is cognitive load theory (Sweller, 1988), which considers that as humans we only have limited working memories and, as such, these can easily be overloaded by too much information or tasks, which are an impediment to the core learning. An example of this is to require pupils to copy some information down from the board to be able to complete a task with them. Some children may find that looking up, remembering the order of the words (particularly if these include new vocabulary or a foreign language) then correctly writing these following the school's handwriting policy actually takes up most of their working memory, leaving them unable to also decide what to do with the information. So do consider when planning what the important aspect of the learning is for that lesson and try to minimise cognitive load.

There are a variety of ways in which you can provide differentiation for your students, including:

- by outcome or response: same lesson for all, pupils answer at their levels, works well with open-ended lessons
- by resource or text: different children have different key supports, e.g. texts that are increasingly complex in language and ideas
- by task: pupils are asked to complete different work (in some schools, pupils can choose themselves which level of questions to answer, or if they complete their work they automatically move on to the next level – a note of caution here: this is not simply an increase in the amount of work, e.g. low ability (LA) groups answer 3 question, middle ability (MA) answer 4, higher ability (HA) answer 6, it's a little bit more nuanced)
- by dialogue: for example, you may choose when framing questions for an EAL (English as an additional language) learner from France to be language conscious and choose cognates
- by support: this is scaffolding by either you as the teacher working with a group or by another adult (be mindful not to place your TA, should you be lucky enough to have one, with your LA all the time – research has shown that it is not always productive to have an assistant, who is usually the least qualified person in the room, helping those with the

most complex needs; you should ensure that support is rotated around the room).

Of course, this is just a whistle-stop tour of differentiation and you will need to understand the needs of your class to ensure that your differentiation is effective for their learning. Planning can be a tricky skill to learn and it can be really useful to look at as many different plans as possible. If you get the chance, ask to see your friends' planning to give you ideas and clarify questions you might have. It is quite reasonable to ask to see your teacher's planning; just be aware that they have 'earned' the right to have quite brief plans through years of detailed careful considerations, whereas you unfortunately are at the start of that journey. However, the important thing to remember, as with all skills that you practise, is that it does get better as you go.

MENTAL HEALTH AND WELLBEING

THINKING ABOUT THOUGHTS

One of the most useful activities that you can do is to reflect on where you are in your teacher education journey. Are there elements that could reasonably be considered to have affected how you are feeling? For example, have you recently changed schools or year groups? Have you increased your teaching timetable or added a new subject with which you are unfamiliar? Perhaps there are issues outside of your placement, such as family situations or financial worries. Of course, all of these things are completely normal, and are in fact part of the vicissitudes of life. Being able to tease worries apart from each other is a really important skill, otherwise sometimes they can become conflated and start to snowball. One of the best ways to be able to do this is to write down on separate post-it notes all of your worries (see other suggestions in Chapter 4). It's really important that you are honest with yourself during this exercise and that you include all of your worries, however silly or unimportant you feel that they are. By doing this you clear out all of the scary, dark thoughts that you might be having and these thoughts are honestly never as bad when out in the light as they are inside your own head.

Once you have all of your thoughts written down, you can start to sort them into groups and consider what sort of action you can take. Some of the worries will simply be sorted by having written them down and you can get rid of these easily. However, some of them will require further work. Once you have separated them out, the first thing that you should do is to consider the difference between your thoughts and feelings, and the evidence that you have for these. This is because sometimes when you are learning new things and having to practise them in front of others and in a public space (e.g. your class, your class teacher and other more senior members of staff) this can leave you feeling a little 'vulnerable'. This is sometimes further compounded by receiving feedback on your academic side as well. Therefore, this is why it can be really helpful to tease out exactly what your thoughts and feelings are as well as considering what 'evidence' you may have for these. It may be that when you are feeling 'exposed' or vulnerable you find that this fear starts to creep into other aspects of your life. A common concern for trainee teachers can be that they feel that their mentor may not like them. Very occasionally, personality clashes can happen; however, most commonly this feeling can come from the trainee feeling overwhelmed, tired and worried. Simply acknowledging this set of circumstances can be enough for many trainees to realise that they need to build in some support or look at making a few tweaks to their work–life balance.

Learning how to challenge an unhelpful thinking style can be useful when training to teach, as it will help you to ensure that you do not fall into distorted thinking patterns. There are different kinds of unhelpful thinking, which we will consider now.

BLACK-AND-WHITE THINKING

This means that your thinking is binary and at either ends of a spectrum. For example, you may feel that the whole lesson that you taught was 'rubbish' or that because you didn't get a first in your essay you're stupid. What can be useful here is to try to look for the 'in-between', as rarely are things just black and white. Therefore, if you consider a lesson, not even a poor lesson would be all bad; if it were you would have documented evidence of this in lesson analysis forms, and your weekly meetings. Furthermore, if the lessons you are teaching are 100 per cent bad then someone would have stopped you from teaching for a while, to enable you to work on this. You could ask the pupils in your class for examples of what they enjoyed or ask your class teacher about what he or she felt was good (the chances are that this has been covered, but you may have been focusing elsewhere).

FILTERING

Filtering is related to back-and-white thinking. This is where you magnify the negative parts and edit out the positives. Again, like when challenging black-and-white thinking, it can be useful to think about the whole picture (including the grey areas). This will take practice, and so asking a friend to help to provide a different perspective can be useful. Alternatively, on a similar note, consider the advice or support that you would give to a friend who was in the same situation. We generally advise our friends in a much more balanced way than we advise to ourselves.

COMPARISONS

Comparisons across your teacher education programme, across other university courses and across institutions is common, especially in social media spaces. When you compare your teaching placement and academic work with others' it can sometimes leave you feeling that you have not achieved as much, as you are only aware of their 'public face'. Social media further heighten this, which really does only present people's carefully scripted public image. Making this comparison can make you feel inadequate. Learning to appreciate yourself and your uniqueness can be much more difficult to develop. For example, you may learn that someone else on your course is only teaching four or five hours a week when you are teaching eight hours and you feel that this is really unfair. In fact, you may not be aware that this is because the other trainee is struggling with their ability to teach and so are on a restricted timetable to enable them to develop. Really, you should try to compare yourself only with yourself, and ask are you teaching as much or as little as you should be given the progress that you are making. If for whatever reason you feel you are not, then this is a legitimate worry.

PERSONALISING

When engaging in personalising thinking this means that you assume the responsibility for everything, whether or not it is actually your fault. In some situations, it will not be your fault and furthermore sometimes there is no fault in situations. Learning to recognise the elements that you have control over, and more importantly those that you do not, is really important in ensuring that you do not simply absorb all the 'blame' yourself. For example, if there is an incident in your classroom, you may feel very guilty if a child is injured. However, if you have taken all due care and attention, and the child was still injured, there is simply nothing that you could have done; sometimes these things happen. If you do find that, in retrospect, there is something that you would do differently, then take this as a learning point for next time you are in the same situation.

MIND READING

It can be tempting to think that we know what other people are thinking, be it our TAs, class teachers or parents. Interestingly, this 'mind reading' only tends to focus in on our negatives. For example, when starting to teach a lesson on a subject that you are not confident in, you may feel that your TA is watching you and judging you. The chances are that they are far too busy with what they need to do to even notice what it is that you are doing. Furthermore, if you have been nervous and revised then even while you still feel worried, you will have improved and learned. In addition, while you are aware of all of this, your TA has no idea. Just because you think something, it does not mean that it is true.

EXAGGERATING

This type of thinking has all possible scenarios ending in some sort of tragic disaster from which you will never recover. For example, what if I don't know the answers? Alternatively, what if the parents ask me a question and I do not know the answer? The chances are that even if things do go wrong the worst thing that can happen is that you are embarrassed. Certainly not the terrible unimaginable outcomes that lurk unchallenged in the darkness of your thoughts.

Challenging unhelpful ways of thinking can be difficult to do, especially if you are tired or feeling emotional. Furthermore, if you have been used to one way of thinking it can be difficult to learn new ways of thinking. However, having read this section you should now be aware of how, between placement, university and other life commitments, you may be falling into one or more of these thought patterns and should this be the case you can always return to this section for support.

CHAPTER SUMMARY

- Do make the effort to go to university – it will stop you from feeling isolated and is a source of support and guidance for your teaching and wellbeing.
- When at university or in training sessions elsewhere, make the most of the discussions and space to ask questions.
- Be clear about what you want your pupils to learn. What will they know, after an hour or so with you, that they didn't already know at the start of the lesson?
- Use Bloom's taxonomy to structure cognitive challenge.

- Do a body and mind scan. Be aware of how you feel and question yourself as to why you might be feeling this way. Then, if you can do something, do it. If not, as Elsa sings, 'Let it go, let it go ...'.
- Be aware of thinking traps.

FURTHER READING

Denby, N. (ed.) (2015) *Training to Teach*, 3rd edition. London: Sage.

A great thematic book, which considers the important aspects of becoming a teacher. Part 2: Strategies for Teaching and Learning is of particular interest.

MacBlain, S. (2014) *How Children Learn*. London: Sage.

This is a superb text, which considers all aspects of how children learn. This book provides you with a really comprehensive overview of how children learn, from which you can base your teaching foundation.

Peters, S. (2012) *The Chimp Paradox*. London: Vermilion.

This is a readable book, which looks at why you might behave like you do and what you can do about your 'inner chimp', how to tame him or her so she or he doesn't derail you.

4

This
CHAPTER
EXPLORES:

- how to write an essay and the importance of reading
- the different approaches to teaching and how to find the one that works for you
- self-care, taking into account the three important foundations: sleep, diet and exercise.

ACADEMIC

HOW TO WRITE THEMATICALLY

This chapter leads on from the section on 'how to read' in Chapter 2. However, should you be on a deadline and have quickly flipped to this section as you have an essay due in and no time to read Chapter 2, let us quickly recap.

You should read widely, which means reading books and journals, and you should start with the reading lists that your university provides. When reading you may have the option to read online or to print, and of course printing can incur a cost. However, you will be able to highlight or anno- tate parts of the article, without having to be attached to an electronic device such as a laptop. This can prove really helpful on placement, if you are maybe reading one journal article a day over lunch. Moreover, printing does give you the option to digitally switch off to complete your reading, whereas if you are reading online the temptation is to look at other con- tent, or to be distracted by notifications. There is also emerging research about how much you really 'take in' when reading from a screen, and this may be a consideration for you. However, there are of course advantages to reading onscreen: you can use the 'find' function to scan texts for key words or terms without having to read the whole document. Whichever way you choose to read, while reading you should note down key concepts or ideas on post-it notes. And then almost as important is keeping these safe. You will know when you have read widely enough and it is time to finish reading as you will start to read about the same concepts time and again, without new information or ideas coming to the fore. This then means that it is time to start writing.

The first point to make is that if you try to start with writing, before you have conducted wide reading, you will find this a tortuous pathway to go down. This is because you have no ideas and are no more informed about your topic than what is already in your head at the start of the process. It is almost guaranteed that some students reading this book will have skipped the section on reading and turned straight to this section, as they are busy and do not have time. This is completely normal; after all writing feels like an action. An action that will get your essay done. Finished. Boxed off. Therefore, you can try to have some down time. However, you should note that reading is also an action. Sure, it is not the star of the show like writing, but trying to write without reading is like building your house on foundations of sand. Furthermore, your writing process will be considerably longer as you have to keep stopping and starting to 'find reading which supports your point of view'.

Of course, you have a choice, but it is very much recommended that if you have not conducted your reading, that you go back, and start to develop some essay writing discipline. In addition, as a side note, this is not in any way your fault, it is probable that no one has ever told you this, or modelled for you how to write an assignment properly. However, it is never too late to learn, you just have to practise.

Depending on previous experiences, students can underestimate how important it is to plan their essays. Alternatively, they may misinterpret this term, and consider that popping in some key terms such as introduction, discussion and conclusion is enough, without populating each of these sections with further ideas. The first step in planning your assignment should be to get your module guide, or assignment handbook or similarly titled document, which tells you about the learning outcomes for your module, the assignment question/title and the marking criteria. In the 'boring' guff at the start of this document it will give you all sorts of information about what you will be studying and how this links to the outcomes and aims of the module and the programmes. Of course, 'busy trainees' do not ever read this; they simply do not have time. Generally, they want to know two things: when do they have to be there and what do they have to do to pass the module. However, when you are writing an essay it can be helpful to understand what the module you are studying is about. Granted, this might be nice to know at the start of the year and would provide you with intrinsic motivation for turning up each week, but no one's perfect. When lecturers write these documents, they have to ensure that the assessment that they create allows each of these outcomes to be measured. There is usually some form of information (table, chart, paragraph) that explains this to you. If you have two assessment points in a module, it will tell you what outcomes are measured through which assessment.

Now that you have the 'big picture', your next step is to look at the essay title/question. Sometimes, these can be a little wordy or long; if this is the case read through it a couple of times, thinking about the outcomes that are measured for this piece of work. Start to consider how you can break down the question into actions and topics. Most questions or titles will require you to 'do something' 'about something'. For example, critically evaluate drama (thing you have to do) as an approach to teaching English (about this thing), or compare and contrast (thing you have to do) Scandinavian and English EYFS settings and their impact on outdoor learning (here there are three things: Scandinavian approaches, English approaches and impact on outdoor learning). By really taking time to understand the question this will ensure that you are aware of what you are trying to answer. So, for example, if we take the question above, some students may be tempted to outline EYFS settings in Scandinavia, EYFS settings in England and then maybe consider outdoor play in the final paragraph. However, few marks will be awarded for the presentation of this material. Most likely, it is your lecturer who has informed you about these settings in the first place, so they do not need you to simply regurgitate it back to them. Instead, you have to use this information to create new learning, through comparing and contrasting. You really have to think, synthesise the information and craft a line of argument. Again, this is where your reading will come in handy, because it is the ideas that snowballed into themes (on your post-it notes) which will act as your paragraphs. So in this example, paragraph topics gathered from the reading might be: outdoor education, length of EYFS phase and government subsidies.

Finally, once you are informed of the 'big picture' and how you are required to demonstrate your knowledge, you should turn your attention to the marking scheme. The person who is charged with marking your assignment will have a copy of the marking scheme in front of them. Pay attention to the verbs and what you need to demonstrate. The example above is again useful to bear in mind, because if the marking scheme says 'is able to demonstrate comparing and contrasting settings' rather than 'is able to present information about settings' then you would not receive marks. The module guide/assignment handbook may contain bullet points for you to consider in your assignment. Generally, these bullet points have been included by your lecturer as points for consideration, rather than individual considerations for you to agonise over and try to include each one into your assignment. If you are unsure of what you need to include, this is where you need to consider the marking scheme again, as this sets out, in black and white, what marks you gain, and perhaps more importantly how to move from one grade boundary to the next.

There may be 'past examples' for you to view before you write. Past papers should have a large note of caution against them as they will provide you with a model of constructing your essay that once seen cannot be unseen. Instead of being able to consider the literally thousands of ways in which you could write your essay, you will instead only have in your mind the one way that you have seen. This can make it very difficult to then put the example essay aside and move on to writing your own essay. After all, the only essay that you can write is your own. The structure, to some degree, is irrelevant as long as you understand the outcomes, the question you are answering and the marking scheme, and so this is where you would be best to spend your time.

Sometimes, referencing is part of the marking scheme. Referencing is as dull as dishwater. As it is so dull and something that you do not participate in doing either willingly or frequently, then each time you are called upon to do it you may find that you cannot remember ever having done it before. While certainly a boring pastime, it is not a difficult one and as such you will simply need to obtain a 'how to reference' guide and sit with it open. There are various different technological solutions to referencing, some being a little better than others, but irrespective of the method you decide to use, just make sure that you are aware of your university's requirements and you stick to them. Do not assume that you know how to reference, and do not assume that just because you know how to reference a book, you know how to reference a website because it changes frequently. If you really have a blank about referencing, go to your library and make an appointment as most will meet you for a one-to-one tutorial, or check your central university offerings as there might be group sessions.

WRITING

Reading, check. Fully briefed about module aims and outcomes, assignment and marking scheme, check. Referencing guide open next to you, check. Right then, yes, you are ready to write. Moreover, your writing process should be considerably more enjoyable and quicker as you have really firm foundations on which you can build.

When you were reading you wrote down key ideas or themes from the texts you were considering. Now is the time to gather together all of your post-it notes. Read each of these quickly and try to notice if groups or themes emerge from them. For example, if you were writing an essay on why we teach foreign languages, you might group together openness of young children, curiosity of kids, naturally inquisitive, learning about others under the theme of intercultural understanding. Alternatively, you may group together financial reward, mobility, economic opportunities, better job prospects under the theme of extrinsic rewards. You may need to go over your post-its a number of times to elicit these themes, and you may need to redistribute some of the post-its as you progress through until you are finally happy with each one. Put all of the post-it notes that contain ideas with the same themes together. Sometimes, you might find that there are too many in one pile, in which case consider whether there are in fact multiple ideas here which you could split up. Or maybe you have only one or two post-it notes in another pile, in which case consider whether these ideas could join another group. It is this group that will form the topics of each of your sections. Of course, the length of an essay dictates how long each section should be, but you should aim to have the main body (everything apart from introduction and conclusion) of the assignment as the largest part and look to split the word count up between these sections, leaving enough words for a short introduction and conclusion section.

Different people have different takes on where to start next. Some people prefer to write the introduction while others prefer to jump straight into the main body of the essay and come back and add the introduction and conclusion later. The approach here favours the latter, because in general an introduction and conclusion never really gain you any marks. They are important as they set the scene for the reader and signpost what will come in the essay and then recap and draw together the threads at the end, so you cannot hand in a piece of work without them. However, you can always add them in at the end once the main body of the essay is completed.

When writing the main body of your essay, this should be approached in sections. For most assignments required on your course two to four paragraphs, which each cover a separate theme, might be appropriate. A theme should be an overarching idea that links the concepts which you are discussing; for example you might choose the theme of discovery learning to discuss science, outdoor learning and maths investigations. The advantage of using themes is that it stops you having to write in a linear way, whereby you would need to write a section on each (science, outdoor learning, maths investigations) and then another section where you link these all together. This means that you have room in your word count for those higher order skills, such as critical analysis or synthesising a line of argument from a selection of sources. Furthermore, because you have had to think about what links all of your ideas from the reading to the post-its to the themes, when you come to write you have a really good understanding of the information.

As you consider starting to write, you may feel that you have not been given enough support from your sessions or lecturers, and sometimes this might be the case. However, quite often students can simply default to this thinking because writing an essay it not easy, it is horrible. It makes your brain hurt, it is a bit boring and quite frankly you would rather be doing something else. It is not a nice experience. It is sometimes made more difficult if, when you last wrote essays as part of an undergraduate course or in sixth form, you were never required to simply 'go it alone' and 'get on with it'. Furthermore, the stakes are high, especially if the grades go towards your final degree classification. Feeling overwhelmed is understandable but there really is nothing a lecturer can say that would make it all completely OK for you, apart from, 'Tell you what, I've a spare afternoon, why don't I write this for you?', which clearly (both having a free afternoon and offering to write assignments) is not going to happen. Joking aside, when you catch yourself feeling overwhelmed by the task you have to complete, it is important to consider that no amount of assignment support would make it an easy or enjoyable activity. So calm yourself by approaching it in a clear, ordered and methodical way. The anxiety that writing an essay produces (for most people not suffering from an anxiety disorder) is the motivation that you need to actually get started and to make you do a good job.

When starting to write there can be nothing more offputting than a blank page; the worry about 'getting it right' or knowing where to start can be crippling for many people. Luckily, for you, you will be writing your assignments on a laptop or computer, rather than quill pen and ink or carving tablets of stone. This is important to remember, because if you make a mistake or you think another section should go before the one you are writing, you can simply cut and paste or delete it. There is no such thing as a perfect essay. There are, however, completed essays and these are nearly as good. So try not to set yourself impossible targets – you simply need to write your essay in the first place and then if you are concerned or worried just go back and edit it. In fact, this is what you should be doing anyway. One final tip, which may be of use, is to open another Word document, let's call it the 'Extra Word Graveyard' (EWG), and this is where, when you come back to review your work, you can cut and paste all the sections and parts that you think on consideration are not actually needed, or required. The reason why these words will go in the EWG rather than simply being deleted is because of the emotional attachment you have made to them over the course of writing your essay. These words represent the hours of evening and weekend work that you have endured and so it can be heart-breaking to just delete them. Instead, pop them into your EWG and you can keep them for ever, and even reinstate them if you change your mind. Although, as sad as it is to see your words find a new home, it may be that it was the right decision and you will never reinstate them.

Achievable targets are really useful in keeping you on track and focused when you are writing. If your target is to write a set number of words before you get to X (play football, shop online, eat a huge bar of chocolate, or go out for drinks that night) it can really ensure that you remain on task. Each time that you find yourself wandering onto Twitter or online shopping, just remind yourself that you have a choice. If you spend time now on other things, it will only delay finishing and enjoying yourself fully as a proper reward knowing that there is no essay at the back of your mind troubling you. This is not an easy frame of mind to enter into and certainly requires practice. However, if you do try you will find you eventually get better at focusing and doing what you need to before taking a break. Just try to ensure that what you are aiming to do is achievable for the time set. Writing an entire essay on a Sunday afternoon is bound to end in failure one way or another.

Once you have written the main body of your essay, it is time to come back to the introduction, which should set the scene for the reader. If you are choosing in the introduction to present some information for the reader, do ensure that you say why this is important to know; your marker will not be a mind reader. Then you should try to signpost for the reader what they can expect in the assignment, so outline the key themes and the order in which they come. Keep the introduction brief and focused. The conclusion should aim to draw together the information that you have presented in the main body and provide the reader with a sense of 'completion'. You are not looking to introduce new concepts here, although you could flag areas that should be considered for research in the future.

Throughout the essay, as a rule, short sentences are better than long ones. Apostrophes are useful as a teacher to model standard English. They are useful in the classroom and they are used to show possession of things in your writing. However, they do not improve work when sprinkled across your essay like glitter on primary school classroom carpet at Christmas. Let us illuminate this further: plurals do not need an apostrophe. Pupil's is something belonging to one child, while pupils' is something belonging to all the kids. And then, there is children's. As it is already plural, the apostrophe comes before the s. There are whole books dedicated to grammar rules and if you are unsure you need to check, not only for your essays but because you could end up teaching your pupils (just a plural) misconceptions. When editing your work try to develop an internal alarm which sounds when you encounter an 's' at the end of a word; then you can ask yourself if it should or shouldn't be there. Much better to be safe than sorry as you start out, but eventually this will become second nature. Finally, activate the spell check and grammar check on your laptop/ computer and if there is a blue/red wavy line under a word, do some further investigations. The main bulk of the marks you will receive will come from meeting the learning outcomes; however, a well-written, easy-to-read piece of work is a rare treat for a lecturer. And while not all your marks will be given for good writing, it certainly doesn't hurt.

Generally when writing an essay it is always better to paraphrase an author or to synthesise their ideas/research into your line of debate. This is because by synthesising the key authors together to craft a line of debate, it is you who is doing the 'heavy lifting'. The chances are that if you are simply presenting quotes, by just plonking them down on the page, you are not really too sure of the point that you are making. It may even be that you have not conducted your reading and have simply googled points to 'back up what you think' and this is your way of demonstrating it. Furthermore, writing in this way means that precious word count is used up on direct quoting when in fact it would be better served really unpicking the why behind the ideas that you are presenting. Again, most universities offer group classes or one-to-one sessions on how to do this successfully. However, ensure that you always acknowledge the words that you used, by including quotation marks around the actual words. Most universities run all academic assignments though a piece of software that can attribute words to their authors. Of course, if you have referenced where these words have come from, this is of course fine (although see above, paraphrasing might be better for a number of reasons). If you have not referenced where the words have come from, at best this is considered to be academic ineptitude and at worst this could be considered plagiarism.

The final job that you need to do before handing in your assignment and having a little relax is to review and edit it. Agreed, the last thing you want to do once you have finished writing is to go back to the start and edit it. However, you do need to because the calm, zen, space which you inhabit once the writing part is done is very different from the anxious, panicked and stressed–out state you were in prior to starting writing. You need to review your work, checking over the boring bits such as grammar and referencing. But more importantly you also need to consider if you have answered the question, as per the marking scheme and the question. Ideally, you'd be checking this as you were writing but a double check at the end is helpful. Sometimes you can be too attached to your work (after all you have written it so you must think it is right) and so swapping with a friend or asking a family member to help you is important. Make sure you ask the right friend because they are not going to relish telling you where to improve or what to take out, and despite what you think, you are not going to want to hear it. However, a good friend will do this for you, and you may just need to learn not to speak up straight away when they give you critical feedback and at all costs resist the urge 'to argue' with them, or you might find you lose a critical friend in the future. Instead have a bank of phrases to use to buy you a bit of time, such as 'Thanks, I hadn't thought of it like that before', or 'I'll have to go away and consider what you've said in a bit more detail'.

There are many ways you can write an essay, but writing a good essay takes a little time. And writing a good essay and not becoming an anxious bag of nerves, who skips lectures and placement while getting it done, can take a bit of trial and error. So in the meantime while you are finding your own route, you could give the above approach some consideration and adapt as you go. But if you always do what you've always done, you'll always get the same thing. And no one likes a frazzled essay loony. Be kind to yourself, get organised and make a plan.

PLACEMENT

MODES OF TEACHING

Modes of teaching is an opaque way of saying: how do you get what is inside your teacher head out so that the learners can do something with it and make meaningful learning inside their own heads? What sorts of teaching do you choose to use? It may be useful to consider modes of teaching as modes of transport; for example, different journeys require different modes of transport best suited to the needs of the passengers and the journey/destination.

Just as you could group modes of transport into air, rail, road and water categories, so too can you group modes of teaching into transmission teaching, transactional teaching and transformational teaching.

Transmission teaching favours a behaviourist approach and can be best seen from the large lecture. This is because it is the teacher who is very much in charge of the teaching and the intended outcomes. This approach favours the idea that there is information held by the teacher which is 'given' to the pupils and they then learn X. In this type of teaching, the teacher controls most variables, including the outcomes. Transmission teaching involves any type of teaching where you are 'presenting' as a one-way street (i.e. there is no interaction with your pupils) so you may do this by telling the pupils the lesson content or the instructions. You could elevate this teaching by including some modelling, examples or pictures using PowerPoint. However, effectively, if you are talking at your pupils, rather than talking with them or listening to them, this is probably transmission teaching. There is of course a time and a place for transmission teaching; however, you as the professional teacher need to decide when this type of teaching is appropriate and when another form might be better.

In contrast to transmission teaching there is transactional teaching. Transactional teaching places the teacher as a learning facilitator (this sounds terrible, and like a job title in a teaching mockumentary but do read on). A learning facilitator organises, sets up and creates learning opportunities for the pupils to interact with and gain learning from. Each student will have a unique outcome, as this learning is linked back to previous experience or knowledge. Therefore, this approach can be viewed through a constructivist lens, or perhaps even a social constructionist viewpoint, as the learners will most likely be interacting with others as well as their tasks and learning environment (Santrock, 2004). Examples of this type of teaching might include discovery learning (Bruner, 1986). This is where you set up the learning in the style of a carousel activity, for example, where all the pupils go from table to table completing activities and tasks with their groups and then at the end of the lesson you bring them all together and they discuss what they have learned. You may participate in the lesson through questioning or eliciting with groups to further probe their thoughts. Of course, the learning in this case will only be as good as the set-up you have created as such transactional teaching is reasonably 'hands off' during most of the lesson, as it is preparation heavy.

The final approach is transformational teaching, which involves more than simply pupils learning the content you either 'transmit' or 'facilitate' them to learn. This approach takes the idea that through learning, individuals can change or transform, either through mindset, approaches to learning or motivation. A commonly cited approach to this type of teaching is Carol Dweck's 'growth mindset'. However, it could be suggested that transformational teaching is much broader and includes character education. Character education may sound a little odd when first encountered, but it is a term which encompasses the teaching of children the knowledge, skills and abilities to help them to develop holistically as a person in society. In fact, you have probably already heard of elements of it, through SMSC (spiritual, moral, social and cultural development). In fact, all schools in England must show how well their pupils develop in SMSC. Character education encompasses SMSC and goes a little wider and as such can include compassion, morality, civic duty, health and hygienic living, critical thinking and questioning.

There are plenty of private companies and websites that offer support for SMSC for schools; however, one of the best resources has to be from the Jubilee Centre for Character and Virtues. It is entirely possible that this name 'turns you off going any further'. This would be a tremendous mistake as quite possibly the way in which you are interpreting this slightly opaque name is certainly not what it is in reality nor what it would actually look like in your classroom. And so if this is the case, stop reading, get out your phone, download the free Jubilee Centre app and have a play-about. A good starting point would be the programmes of study which illustrate for you why and how you can achieve character education within your classroom. Should the name have not put you off reading, it might be useful at this point to know that the goal of character education is an even less clear term called eudemonia. Simply put this is living well and studying well, in a nutshell flourishing, and as a teacher this is what you would like to achieve for your pupils. Not just simply sat there, bored to tears on a Tuesday afternoon, but engaged and inquisitive because they love learning and want to apply it in the real world for an actual purpose that engages them. The Jubilee Centre (2018) explains that 'the pathway to [eudemonia] is the acquisition and development of virtues and it is the virtues we have acquired which go to make up our character. A virtue is the ability to act in a particular way in a specific situation to bring about a good outcome.' The Centre goes on to explain that 'virtues such as courage, kindness, persistence, love of learning and self-discipline are all around us – to varying degrees – in us and in the lives of the people we know. When we have acquired a virtue, we become able to manage our emotions and give reasons for why we choose a particular course of action; we learn to deliberate and assume much more control over how we act in the circumstances we face.' Depending on your own philosophy about education, this may be to varying degrees important to you. However, it is interesting to note at this point that all forms of hate crime have increased in England since 2015. Furthermore, internationally there has been a shift from multicultural policies to monoculture protectionist policies with a number of far-right parties having been elected across the world. Within the media, many forms of nuance seem to have been lost; for example, have you ever considered the difference between economic migrant, refugee or asylum seeker (as these terms are used quite interchangeably in the media, but represent varying degrees of plight, trauma and desperation to find a safe space for themselves and their loved ones)?. It may now seem that this chapter has veered off on a very different tangent to modes of teaching; however, it is important that the children whom you teach are equipped to understand, question and act as sensitive, informed individuals who are capable of critical thinking. And this is where character education comes into play. The ability of children to understand the world around them, while also learning the curriculum, is key in creating a fair and respectful world for all. The difficulty comes as a teacher because 'measurements of teaching' rarely, in meaningful ways, measure character education. It would be remiss to move on from this chapter without giving a brief mention of 'British Values', which are often taught through SMSC. The term 'British Values' has always been a slightly odd one, as it could give the impression that these values are in some way exclusively British. 'British Values' have been defined by Ofsted as 'democracy; the rule of law; individual liberty; mutual respect for and tolerance of those with different faiths and beliefs and for those without faith'. However, it is quite clear to see that these are in fact 'human values'. Human values might have been a better, more inclusive, term, which invites everyone to celebrate and share in what makes us all similar, rather than the exclusive term 'British Values', which seems to pit 'us' against 'them'. Back to the Jubilee Centre for Character and Virtues, it is important to note that there is a range of free resources for you to use online or download via the app. However, what is really nice is that these are mapped in a progressive and coherent approach from reception right through primary and even into the secondary programme. It is rare to see such a well-thought-out, planned and joined-up approach. And even rarer to see it for free.

This section does not advocate one method of teaching over another, nor one mode. And the resources recommended are certainly not the only resources, but they are a good starting point. Hopefully from this you can be more aware of the range of teaching theories, approaches and ideas that exist and from this you will create your own magic blend for the children in each of your classes. A word of caution should be noted here: you will never be able to use exactly the same magic blend on more than one class. While you might use some of the main ideas, each class is a unique organism which individually and collectively behaves differently from the last class that you had. Even if you have the same class for two years running, you'll need to update because your children have been updated. It is through having a research-informed approach and being aware of the multiplicity of ideas and theories, and reflecting on these in practice, that you can become a professional teacher. And so this is what should drive you and inspire you to attend university when it's dark and cold outside, you have a billion things to do for placement and that 9 a.m. lecture seems like a 'waste of time; it isn't, it's going to be another magical ingredient for your very own style of awesome teaching.

MENTAL HEALTH AND WELLBEING

OFFICIALLY KNACKERED – HOW TO RECHARGE

In Chapter 2, the idea was introduced that you move from being unconsciously incompetent, to consciously incompetent, before becoming consciously competent and then finally unconsciously competent. However, what Chapter 2 did not focus on was how this might affect your mental health and more importantly what you could do to support yourself through your teacher training. Being unconsciously incompetent is glorious; you have no idea of what you do not know, and obviously unconsciously competent is the desired state. However consciously incompetent and consciously competent are difficult stages of your training, made particularly worse if this stage corresponds with the clocks going back and it being dark all time. This can lead trainee teachers to disengage with university sessions, to fall behind with expectations on placement, and then to feel that there is simply no way to get back on track and see the only solution as quitting the course. Therefore, this section is designed to help you when you find yourself in a difficult time in your teacher training, by offering some practical steps that you could take. The advice in this section is not revolutionary and it may be made up of ideas you are already familiar with; however, sometimes just seeing advice written down in an actual book legitimises your ideas and prompts you to actually act on your own advice. Finally, this section also legitimises those difficult times; what you are experiencing is, for want of a better word, 'normal' from time to time. Should you find yourself in what Dr. Seuss (1990) labels a 'slump', remember that 'this too shall pass'. However, should you find that you are worried or that your difficult time is extending for longer than you feel is reasonable then this is the point at which you should really start to seek help.

Let us now look at three basic foundations to 'self-care'. The foundations are sleep, diet and exercise, and the place to start is sleep.

SLEEP

If you are worried, you may find that you start to experience issues with your sleep. You may find it difficult to fall asleep with an overactive mind or to stay asleep during the night as you are worrying. However, just as worries can cause sleep issues, so too can lack of sleep contribute to feelings of anxiety and low mood. It can be a difficult trap to extract yourself from. Everyone has different levels of sleep that they need. However, lack of sleep does mean that you will experience difficulty maintaining concentration and lack motivation, two essential skills required for teacher training. Sleeplessness may also cause you to feel listless and irritable, which if you worked in isolation in a computer booth may be tolerable but when faced with thirty pupils all day might just be a step too far. So what can you do to improve your sleep?

One of the things you can do is ensure that your bedroom is a quiet, dark, distraction-free room. Do not take work into your bedroom, eat in your bedroom or be on your phone. Your brain has to associate your bedroom with switching off. The phone suggestion in this list may have caused some surprise, but the last thing you need before bed is the blue light from a phone screen or the entire world at your fingertips. Your brain cannot distinguish between 'fight and flight' responses for real actual threats and similar anxiety-inducing responses to conflicting posts or ideas on the Internet. Nor do you need minute-by-minute trauma-inducing news delivered to your bedside. Do your amygdala (part of your brain which can run away with you emotionally) a favour, turn your phone on to silent and try disengaging with it at least thirty minutes to one hour before bed. Try to keep your bedroom slightly cooler than the rest of the house and have a warm bath/shower before bed. Research shows that the drop in body temperature after a warm bath/shower can promote sleep.

You should also try to limit your caffeine intake. We all know that caffeine is a teacher's friend, but try to limit your caffeine intake during the daytime and maybe switch to decaffeinated in the afternoon, as this is a stimulant. It is the same with nicotine, so try to limit smoking before you go to bed. Alcohol, used in moderation, can help you to fall asleep. However, please note that alcohol is a depressant and can also affect the quality of the sleep that you get when you do drift off. Therefore, you would be better swapping that wine for an alternative and keeping it as a treat, rather than a sleeping aid/ working-week crutch because in the long term this will do you more harm than good.

Try as much as possible to keep to a routine. By setting a regular sleep schedule, your body can get into a pattern and know when to 'expect' sleep. This means having a dedicated time for working when you get home from school, but also ensuring that work does not spill out of this time. Occasionally of course, this may happen, but most of the time you should try to block off time for working and time to relax before you go to bed. Fitness trackers, smart watches, etc. can be useful in reminding you about this and helping to track what sleep you actual get versus what you think you get.

When rushing between placement, university and family commitments it can be difficult for you to have time to really consider what is troubling you. Keep your post-it notes with you, and if you have a quiet five minutes try to put your phone down so you are not distracted, and really think about how you are feeling. Jot down any issues or worries you might have. Then when you have a little longer you can consider these as discussed above. This means that you can start to address your worries as they arise rather than letting them build up. Furthermore, if you are slightly anxious it can be tempting to put off consider-ing what is bothering you, only really beginning to do this once the feelings become 'too much'. Better to do this earlier rather than later and then things will not get on top of you. Hopefully, this means that when you do get into bed to go to sleep you have already considered the issues which were bothering you, allowing you to go straight to sleep. However, should you find you are troubled by other concerns, keep a notepad by you bed, note them down and deal with them in the morning.

If the dealing with worries strategy as outlined above does not appeal to you, why not invest in some Guatemalan worry dolls. There are about five to seven little people in the box, and the idea is you tell each of them one of your worries as you get into bed. This is a great technique as you can only have five to seven worries so it forces you to consider what is really bothering you. And then you have to verbalise your worries, succinctly to 'another'. The simple trick of vocal-ising what is worrying you is such a powerful tool, as it gets the worry out of the darkness of your mind and into the open. They always seem much less 'big' when out. Then you place the dolls under your pillow and they deal with your issues for you while you sleep.

Find time in your day, even if it is only five minutes, to try to relax. You are probably thinking that is not possible. But you should have five minutes breathing space in a day. You need to recharge and regroup, to ensure that you can 'go the distance'. A teacher training course is a marathon, not a sprint. Learning how to 'future proof' yourself for the difficult times is especially important when on a busy teacher training course, otherwise one day your head will simply explode. OK, that last bit is not entirely true. Nevertheless, consider if you constantly run any kind of motor without turning it off – how long it would last? It would get too hot, too quickly and an auto stop function would kick in. You too need to prioritise yourself (self-care again). The speed and quality of the work that you get through and produce when rested and well is considerably more and better than when you are 'swimming through treacle'. Sometimes, you have to take time, to make time. Don't believe me? That's OK, then maybe consider the work of researchers in this area such as Wendy Suzuki and Joseph LeDoux to name two at the University of Oxford Mindfulness Centre, and then reassess your judgement. You are of course quite right to be a little sceptical of the term mindfulness, as it seems to have been 'hijacked' by the wellness industry and attached to pretty much everything and anything.

If you do find that there are nights that you simply cannot sleep and are wide awake, try getting out of bed. Tempting as it might be to turn on your phone, do not engage with this piece of technology as it is just too stimulating. Instead, undertake another relaxing activity such as reading or listening to music. When you start to feel sleepy again, go back up to bed. Hopefully this will mean that you form positive associations with your bedroom and sleep.

DIET

The next foundation for you to consider is your diet. When you are busy, diet can often be the area of your life that you neglect and you may opt for less than healthy options and there can be fewer healthy places than the average staffroom. This is not to say that you cannot indulge in the odd well-earned treat, but these unhealthy options should be a treat and not the norm. Following an 80/20 rule can be helpful whereby you aim to eat healthily 80 per cent of the time, with the 20 per cent reserved for Friday afternoon after class X following wet break. This is because quite often these quick fixes are high in calories, saturated fat and salt while also being low in the essential nutrients that you need. There is some evidence to suggest that a poor diet can exacerbate feelings of anxiety and that eating well can assist feelings of being well. After all, you are what you eat. Specific nutrients that may be beneficial for anxiety disorders include vitamins such as folate, vitamin B12 and choline; minerals such as magnesium and zinc; omega-3 fatty acids; the amino acid tryptophan (precursor of serotonin); and antioxidants such as vitamin E, C, carotenoids and flavonoid polyphenolics. If you want a healthy diet, shop around the outside of the supermarket, do not go into the middle aisles. Eat more vegetables than you think you should do, and less sugar than you think you should, and try to cut back on processed food. Try to eat a rainbow diet and drink more water. It really is that simple, but food manufacturers simply would not make so much money out of you if this was the more promoted route. One of the easiest ways to ensure that you eat well at school and at a home is to batch cook. When cooking meals, you could make a little extra, and then freeze these meals. Please make sure you label these frozen meals, to avoid playing meal roulette. With a well-stocked freezer of meals, you can simply grab something in the morning and go.

EXERCISE

The next area to consider is exercise. Exercise has been shown to be really effective in helping to stay feeling mentally well. Of course, it is difficult to manage to complete all your placement work, university work and sort out your family obligations and then still have time for exercise. One of the ways in which you can do this easily is by trying to build it into your day, so it does not become 'just one more thing for you to do'. For example, once or twice a week when you are not returning sets of books back to school, you could try parking ten minutes away from school and building steps into your day. After lunch you could also set aside a little time to go for a walk, or do five minutes skipping in the playground. Not only will the exercise do you good but also simply being outside is good for you, because despite driving cars, living in houses and operating computers a human is still an animal. A combination of effects on the senses provides feelings of wellbeing for people; even just drinking your morning coffee in the garden for fifteen minutes has been shown to have an impact. If you are interested in this, for both you and the children you teach, you might like to research the term *shinrin-yoku*. This is a Japanese term which means 'forest bathing'. In Japan, this is a very common form of preventative health care and it is making inroads in the UK too for adults and children alike. Consider a recent report that stated: '12% of all children (c. 1.3 million) normally never visited the natural environment in the preceding 12 months' (Hunt, Burt and Stewart, 2015: 1). So it might just benefit both you and the children to start getting out more, even if it is just a quick five minutes skipping at lunch or breaktime. Like it or not, you are a role model for the children that you teach. Chances are, if you start this 'challenge', by the end of the week you will most likely be met by a merry band of pupils skipping too. You may be lucky enough that your school is part of the Daily Mile challenge, whereby pupils run or jog for fifteen minutes, so get your PE kit on and join in.

Setting yourself a challenge with a date in the future is also a good motivator. It does not have to be an Iron Man; you can instead do a 1k fun run, or take part in a sponsored event. The 'Couch to 5k' is a great app to get you up and active in a very progressive manner. But the important step is telling friends you signed up. Being held accountable is very motivating and will help to keep you on track. You may want to do this with others on your course; again research shows this is a successful way of keeping going over time.

Of course, if you are feeling overwhelmed and tired, finding the energy to overcome this is a Herculean effort. If this is the case for you, you first need to recognise where you are, and by taking this first step you can begin to help yourself. Sit down and make a plan to participate in one exercise session for the week coming and then, irrespective of how you feel, make yourself go and participate. It's always easier if you have a friend going with you, as you'd never want to let them down. Let's be clear though, the most difficult aspect is the going; once there you will be fine and afterwards you'll be proud of yourself with a sense of achievement and some kickass feel-good hormones floating around in you. So do take a minute afterwards to consider how you feel, as you may feel physically better, mentally clearer and proud of yourself for going. You need to remember that feeling for the next time you do not feel like going. Eventually, if you practise doing this it will become a habit.

This section is designed to consider actions you could take and to empower you to support yourself by creating and maintaining firm foundations. The ideas and suggestions above should be considered preventative measures, akin to taking care of your teeth. Hopefully, if you take good care of your teeth, you shouldn't have to see your dentist regularly for treatments. Sure, every now and again you might need a little 'fixing up' but hopefully you avoid the 'major stuff' by being proactive. So try to embed these foundations into your life. They won't prevent you from having difficult times, but they may help you to get back on track. While all trainee teachers might experience peaks and troughs of emotions during training, these troughs will pass. However, if you find yourself stuck in a 'low' which doesn't seem to be showing any signs of passing you should contact your university support services as well as going to see your GP, because sometimes you may need a little more support than you can provide on your own. If you do require further support, it is not a binary choice; you can practise these suggestions alongside treatments that you are recommended.

CHAPTER SUMMARY

- Read more than you think you should; and then read a little more.
- Spend time planning thematically and the writing then takes care of itself.
- Consider how you are teaching: is it engaging? Could it be done in a different way? Why did you choose that approach for that lesson over another?
- Sleep, eat a healthy diet, exercise, repeat. And if you 'fall off the wagon' one day, simply get back on the next day. It's not about practising for sainthood, but consider it more an 80/20 balancing act of healthy approaches versus binge watching box sets, stuffing pizza in your face and guzzling Lambrini.
- By and large, if something is marketed as healthy, it isn't. An apple or broccoli do not require a huge sticker on them advertising the benefits, and you simply will never see an egg labelled 'extra protein'. Of course not, that would be bonkers. Genuinely healthy food markets itself.

FURTHER READING

The Detective Dot books by Bright Little Labs.

This series introduces children to basic coding while also having an eye on tackling stereotypes for children and also promoting criticality. This sounds like a horrendously difficult and complex gig to pull off, but they do this very well indeed, and if I were teaching computing these days I would be requesting some Detective Dot books in the library. I know that they are currently looking to develop some curriculum materials for schools, so keep an eye out for these. The Detective Dot books are some of the few books I've hungrily read from start to finish, which these days is no mean feat, but I thoroughly enjoyed them.

Morgan, E. (2016) *Anxiety for Beginners*. London: Bluebird.

A personal account of one woman's journey with and into anxiety, in all its forms, as well as the science behind treatments. The book unpicks and gets to grips with what mindfulness actually is and the reasons why it works. The whole book is an interesting read, but the chapter on mindfulness in particular stood out for me. She recommends, if you are interested, searching for key terms MBSR, MT or 'compassion and awareness' (Morgan, 2016: 308) to ensure you find the 'right' kind of mindfulness training.

Meditainment: www.mediament.com

A website that has guided meditations which can link to the Lumi alarm clocks and 'read' to you as you go to sleep. A Lumi alarm clock is much nicer than a 'beep beep beep' in the dark, as it gradually glows lighter and you can set the wake-up tone to something altogether more cheery such as birds singing. Actual Lumi alarm clocks are a little on the expensive side, but in recent years both Aldi and Lidl have brought out their own versions, though these do not link to the guided meditations.

The Best Thing since Sliced Bread? podcast

This BBC Radio 4 podcast looks at the science behind many of the 'wellness industries food' claims. So far with the help of an army of scientists, it has looked at the purported health claims of turmeric, kombucha and vitamin C among others, and in the final considerations of each show, they confirm if the 'super food' is indeed the best thing since sliced bread or if in fact it is all marketing hype.

5

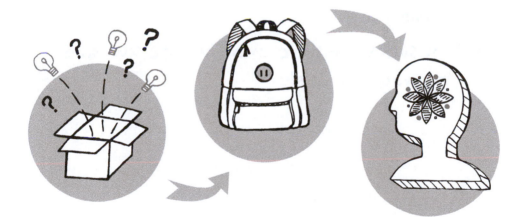

This
CHAPTER
EXPLORES:

- why you should attend seminar sessions and how to make the most of them
- the return to placement after a break and how to assess your own journey so far
- how social media can influence you and the way you feel.

ACADEMIC

MAKING SEMINARS AND SMALL GROUPS WORK FOR YOU

As part of your initial teacher education you are likely to participate (or, perhaps on the odd occasion, slink in late at the back of the room and hope to be ignored) in a variety of different types of sessions. Many universities use a mix of large lectures to first present the baseline information that students need to know before moving on to explore this information in context during a seminar. Sometimes, students may think, 'But what's the point? Just tell us what we need to know and then we can leave, and get on with our marking/planning/essay writing [delete as applicable].' If only it were that simple.

In order to understand university sessions more deeply, you have to start with the question: what are you are paying your tuition fees for? If it were as simple as being told something and then leaving, then to be honest you could probably just google whatever it was you wanted to know and save yourself the time, money and hassle of attending a university in the first place. It would be useful to now consider what the main aims of lectures and seminars really are.

Lectures are, generally, to present the headline information; they usually involve large groups and as such tend to provide 'pre-packaged information'. 'Pre-packaged' means that the content is usually decided in advance, and then presented. This information is given in lectures so that in a seminar you can start to play about with it and apply it in your particular setting and context. So what is it about attending seminar sessions that can be so beneficial? There are eight top reasons, including:

1   A seminar has a rough sort of a road map, but because they are designed to engage and encourage participation, the actual pathway to the outcomes are created by you. This means that you have the chance to ask your questions and see what your peers and tutors think. On many occasions, asking these questions gives you the chance to find out what you *actually* think. Sure, you have an approximate idea, but until those words come out of your mouth, you can never be entirely sure. Furthermore, defending and/ or altering your opinions further refines and clarifies who you are and your teaching philosophy.

2   Linked to the first point, by developing how you feel about teaching, you develop as a reflective practitioner (Schön, 1987). A reflective practitioner is someone who considers what happened and why, looking to improve or understand practice. In your evaluations of teaching this is what you are meant to do, although sometimes at the end of the day you will, quite honestly, put any old sentence in those boxes, just cross that job off the to do list. Teachers and trainee teachers are some of the busiest people on earth (DfE, 2014), and so the opportunity to sit and actually talk about what has happened in school and how this relates to theory is important. Which brings us on nicely to the next point.

3   Moving from a reflective practitioner to a reflexive practitioner. If a reflective practitioner reviews and considers what happened and why, a reflexive practitioner then goes on to make plans to improve/change practices (Stîngu, 2012). Sometimes, this can be tricky as you are used to seeing things through your own lens and it can be a struggle to try to imagine how you might approach the same concept in a different way (Brookfield, 2005). Fear not. This is exactly what a seminar is there for, the chance to discuss and share ideas. A good seminar will make your teaching life easier and less lonely.

4   Bridging the gap between theory and practice is not always easy. Sure, you can know what all those behaviourists did with their animals and children (Skinner and rats, Thorndike and cats, Pavlov and his dogs, and not to mention Watson, Rayner and poor little Albert) but what does that mean for you in your class with your kids on a Tuesday afternoon after wet play? Seminars can act as the bridge between the research and your practice. Your lecturer will know that you are familiar with the work of Vygotsky (1978), namely 'scaffolding' or to

give it its proper title the 'Zone of Proximal Development'. This is what is at play in your seminars; your lecturer facilitates you to achieve and understand more than you could on your own reading about an abstract theory. It might be worth noting that this is, of course, the same idea in play when you get home and start to work independently and discover that all of the ideas, which you completely understood in class, now seem utterly baffling again.

5   Have you heard of the term social media 'echo chambers'? It means that you only tend to follow, retweet, read, etc. people who have similar views and outlooks to yourself. This makes perfect sense: why would you follow someone whose political/economic or gender views enrage and upset you (although Internet trolls *are* the exception)? This means that you can be surrounded by views that are the same as your own. Instead of the Internet making us all more diverse and aware of differing views, actually we may surround ourselves with similar views and, as such, our perception of the world may become somewhat skewed. However, attending a seminar gives you a chance to hear differing views from your own, to hear different methods of teaching and curriculum organisation. Moreover, if you are savvy you'll make notes, make friends and stop reinventing the wheel.

6   In a seminar, you will learn that everyone is worried about something. It is not just you. Trainee teachers at whatever stage of their journey are one of the loveliest groups of individuals I have ever met; that said, they do love a good worry. I think, this worrying comes from wanting to do a good job. Seminars provide you with the chance to get these worries out in the open and you will find it's not just you. In addition, they give you the chance to hear 'realistic' tales of 'out in the field', rather than the 'Instagrammable' face that most people maintain. A good seminar should follow AA rules, 'what you hear here, when you leave here, let it stay here'. By following this rule, everyone can feel comfortable sharing what they are interested in, worried about or proud of regarding their teacher training journey.

7   As touched upon in point number 5, seminars facilitate you to make new friends and 'borrow' their planning, resources and references for essays. Now, to be clear here, I am not advocating plagiarism. This is where you take someone else's words and pass them off as your own (Blum, 2009). This is obviously completely unacceptable in the academic community. However, what I am proposing is that you share some of the 'heavy lifting'. Teachers do this *all* the time. There is no need to completely do everything on your own – that way utter madness lies. OK, not quite, but you will not have a social life, friends or family. Communities of practice

(Wenger, 1998) are what you are looking to develop, and these can go on to sustain you as you enter your first teaching position.

8   In seminars, you have the opportunity to develop relationships with your tutors. Big lecture-theatre teaching has its own rewards, but two-way interaction is not one of them. They are rather like attending a stand-up gig. Your lecturer will try to convey the important information while at the same time attempting to entertain and keep the hecklers at bay (the most common form of this in a large group is the quiet, yet just as disruptive phones sneaking out). In terms of actual interaction from the audience, it is limited. In a seminar, you are able to have a real chat with your tutor, find out a bit about them and they start to understand you more. This is important because it helps to personalise your learning (see point 1). In seminars, because they are small, everyone becomes a 'real person', as does your lecturer. Sometimes you can learn more from chatting to your lecturer about their experiences than in the seminar. Now, it may be that at this point you are thinking, 'Well, this is all well and good, but I've not got time to be making friends and chatting to tutors! Just tell me the information.' That would be fine if you were a robot, but you're not. You are a human being and, as such, the social context to learning is important. It is beneficial to be part of a small group to help you to feel accepted and included at university. It is easy to miss sessions and think that you'll just catch up from friends or from the VLE, but you miss the social experience of sitting with folk who are all going through the same thing as you. Even if you cannot stand your seminar group, it is still a social experience. This may sound cheesy and as if a seminar group can cure any problem, and sometimes it will. However, not attending certainly does not solve any of the issues you may face. Students who do not attend sessions perform worse in academic work as well as experiencing a sense of isolation from their peers (even if they do find them annoying).

Now that we have covered *why* you should attend a seminar group, let us now look at *how* to make the most of your time once there. Many seminar groups will require you to do some form of learning in advance. Your tutor will do this to maximise the learning time, so you do not have to spend twenty minutes of a single hour's session silent reading with your peers. If this advanced preparation seems like too much work some weeks, why not split the workload across you and your friends and then share the highlights with each other? Of course, it is entirely possible to turn up without having prepared anything, but consider how that preparation might help later with planning or essays. However, prepared or not, once you are in the seminar session be prepared to get involved. Simply turning up and hoping to learn is like buying a gym membership and going to watch other people training.

Learn to ask your questions in real time, not at the end of the session. The chances are that if you are thinking about a topic and would like further information or clarification there are probably at least two other people in your group thinking about the same thing, but too worried to ask. It may help to know that when I started lecturing, at the end of each session I would always ask, 'Does anyone have any questions?' Everyone would stay quiet. I would then say, 'I'm flattered, but I'm not sure I'm that good of a teacher that no one has any questions'. The students would politely laugh (and I would die a little inside, as I would have loved them to have corrected me) and then the session would end. A small queue would form of students each with the same or similar questions. I have now learned over the years how to get these questions out into the open during a seminar and try to base the seminar around these questions. So do please remember, *it is not just you.*

In general, maximising your seminar sessions comes back to developing the ability to speak in front of other people. This, you may think, is a key skill of the primary teacher. There you would be wrong. Trainee primary teachers are a funny old bunch; they will quite happily chat to a room full of little children, but a room full of adults is their Kryptonite. Some students may find doing a presentation to just one tutor a real challenge, so it is not even the number of adults that is the issue. So, then, how do you go about getting better at speaking out? Consider some non-teaching examples. How would you plan to improve at playing the piano? How would you become more proficient at riding a bike? (You may have a feel for where we are going here, but let's persist with one more example.) How would you get better at modelling your school's hand writing policy? Yes – of course, you would practise. You may play some dud keys in a tune, or you may even fall off your bike, and when writing on an interactive whiteboard, those letters are simply never going to look like the policy states first time. And all of this is OK. Developing confidence to share your ideas, thoughts and feelings is really a key skill at university seminars. A seminar is not like Twitter where you may receive a backlash, nor is it like your social group who may just always agree with you – seminars are somewhere in the middle. You will make mistakes, get the wrong end of the stick and perhaps reveal some insecurities. But the upside of doing all of these 'cringey things' is that you (The Brave One) will be continuously improving, changing and reshaping your practice and ideas. This will give you confidence that what you are doing is heading in the correct direction, and that you have helped some of your classmates who are struggling with the same ideas. Therefore, if you get it 'wrong' you develop confidence and learn, and if you get it 'right' you develop confidence and learn; remember, every day is a school day. Do please note, you will have to try, and you might feel uncomfortable, but actually this is pretty much the worst that will happen to you and there really is so much to be gained. Remember, as Christopher Robin said to Winnie the Pooh 'You're braver than you believe, and stronger than you seem, and smarter than you think'.

PLACEMENT

NEW YEAR, NEW YOU – CORRECTING PREVIOUS MISTAKES AND WHAT TO DO WHEN IT STILL GOES WRONG

Returning to placement after a break can be the chance to take a step back, assess your placement experience and then consider how you might play it differently (or further embed good practice). One of the best ways to audit yourself before returning to placement is to consider the following suggestions.

SPEAK TO FRIENDS

Take time to speak to friends and try to investigate what placement looks like for them. Please note, there can be no standard day. Your teaching times, mentor styles and children may all be different, so try not to be too hung up on these differences and any perceived unfairness. Instead, try to understand how they approach placement. What do they do when they do not understand something? Who do they go to for support? How did they find out about a topic? What do they do when they teach a 'poor' lesson? What do they do when they teach a 'great' lesson? How do they know what is a 'poor' and what is a 'great' lesson? How do they manage marking/planning/assessment/clubs? How do they handle receiving feedback which they don't agree with? By asking these questions, you will learn about the thought processes someone else uses to support themselves on placement. If you do not ask these questions, you will only ever see the end product of their actions, but not the thoughts which helped to deliver them. Exploring your awareness of your own thoughts as well as others' internal processes is called metacognition and can help to reveal different methods of approaching ideas (Meichenbaum, 1985). As a side note, using metacognition to scaffold the thinking of your students and tease out ideas from them is helpful for all in your class (Education Endowment Foundation Teaching and Learning Toolkit).

LISTENING AND ACTING ON ADVICE

You may or may not like your mentor and/or class teacher. It may surprise you to learn that is irrelevant. Of course, it is probably much better for everyone involved if you do have a rapport, but this is not a prerequisite to making progress. What you do need to acknowledge and accept is that your mentor/class teacher is an experienced professional, and your teaching guide. It can be tricky to overcome the feeling that their choices (teaching topics, resources, groupings, etc.) might not be the same as yours. If you have the time, when you come up against these 'mini-conflicts' consider writing them down. Then, when you get your own class, you can begin to implement your own ideas. Furthermore, this notebook may serve as a useful reminder, when you start to mentor students, of differing approaches. In the meantime, while you are a 'squatter' in someone else's classroom you do need to follow advice. On a serious note, the class teacher carries the responsibility for the progress or lack of progress that the children make. This means that being given the chance to practise in another teacher's classroom with his or her children is a privilege. It can be frustrating because you have your own ideas, values and experiences that you would like to implement. Just try to be patient. When you have your own class, the decisions will all be yours (in line with the school's approach, of course, and the government's National Curriculum) but you may find you wished you had someone making at least some of the decisions for you.

On the same topic, perhaps the way in which your mentor communicates with you is not how you would, in an ideal world, like it to be. As considered above, this is part of being human, rather than a clean, clinical robot. We all, sometimes, play it wrong. Being able to see past this and act on advice and feedback (even if it is not what you would like to do) is a key strength for trainee teachers. The ability to listen and act on advice is the single biggest predictor of overall teaching success. This means that you continuously learn, develop and improve throughout your teaching career (Dweck, 2006).

However, if you feel there really is an issue, which sits outside of the 'norm' in the first instance, it can be really helpful to learn how to raise this with your mentor. Being able to have difficult conversations as a professional is all part of becoming a teacher. If this is an area you feel you need to develop, it might be worth taking time to consider communication styles and to develop a more assertive style. This means you will be able to discuss how you feel on placement as things arise without feelings building up and you starting to carry resentments.

PLATE SPINNING

Each time you go back to placement, usually the demands and/or expectations increase: more teaching hours, teaching different subjects, a new Key Stage or even a change of schools. Managing to keep all of the plates spinning is a real skill. To master 'plate spinning' you need to be organised with daily, weekly and monthly jobs. Then you need to make a plan and stick to it, irrespective of how you feel, because if you do not want to mark thirty books today, then you will not want to mark sixty tomorrow. The difficulty comes in developing the discipline to carry out the plan. It sounds so simple, but if you have a set of jobs to do, make sure that once you have completed them you have something lovely planned to do afterwards. This also helps to keep you focused when doing the job, so your mind and your focus do not find their way over to something altogether more interesting on the Internet. Acknowledging that there will always be something more engaging on the Internet is key, but as you have your 'lovely activity' planned so you'll be able to focus on this. Some people like to use paper-based methods of organisation such as to do lists, diaries and calendars. This can work really well; however, they do rely on you going to the 'paper'. An alternative method is to use your preferred technology, and to programme in events, and the lead-up to events. For example, if you have planning due in on a Friday, it can be worthwhile adding a reminder for Wednesday at 4.30 p.m. to do planning and a safety net reminder on Thursday at 7 p.m. so that by Friday it is done. The nice thing about this approach is that once all dates and tasks are planned for the week/month/year, you can then relax and these things 'come to you'. Where this approach falls down is that it is only as good as the inputting.

BEING PROACTIVE

Being proactive can mean demonstrating leadership where possible (e.g. you might be a fantastic artist, so you could offer to run an art club;

you may have had previous experiences teaching languages, in which case you could offer your skills to team teach with your class teacher or develop topic-based lessons with language links). It also means seeking help when you need it, in a timely fashion. It involves being organised enough to predict possible issues that may arise and then seeking support, in advance, to overcome these. Sometimes students find the predicative element of this a little tricky. They cannot effectively horizon scan, and therefore may encounter problems and at the very last minute ask for help, perhaps not taking into consideration the workloads of other members of staff. This is why developing organisational skills as a teacher is so important. These skills allows you to see where you may have future issues, and to seek support, without compromising others.

NOT ENJOYING OR THRIVING ON PLACEMENT?

Sometimes despite all best attempts, you may not be enjoying or thriving on placement. This section offers practical guidance and steps to consider to help you to determine the source of this feeling.

It is possible that you are not enjoying/thriving on placement for a variety of reasons, and these can be divided into two categories: those pertaining to yourself and those pertaining to the placement. Sometimes, it can be a mix of both. A useful exercise is to write down your concerns under the headings 'personal' and 'placement'. This will enable you to see clearly where the issues you are experiencing are stemming from. All too often when busy, tired and on the go our feelings can become all mixed, and you may feel that these concerns all stem from the same place, but when it is written down in front of you the picture actually becomes much clearer. The next step is to look at which of these concerns you can take action to improve. If you find that there are many on the list that are beyond your control, it may be worth discussing a leave of absence with your provider until some of these issues resolve themselves (managing illness, caring responsibilities, etc.). If you are not able to engage in placement fully, but also feel it is worth persevering for a little while longer, rather than taking a leave of absence, there is plenty of support that can be implemented in the interim. It is always worth talking with your provider or your class teacher or both if you have good relationships. Over the years, the schools with which my colleagues and I work have encountered all kinds of issues and there really is nothing that surprises us anymore. However, there is always something that can be done to support students, although we do have to be aware that there is a problem in the first place. Possible types of support that could be put in place include your PPA being arranged to enable to you to access appointments or other service. Perhaps essay deadlines could be extended to ease pressure on placement, or your placement could be shortened/extended as per need.

Reasons often given for not enjoying placement do differ from reasons for not thriving on placement, although lack of enjoyment can underpin why a trainee may not excel on placement. Quite often, the number one concern is work–life balance. It is important to realise that in teaching there will be peaks and troughs, and that the expectation of a 'flat year-long' cycle simply is not realistic. The problem may lie in the fact that there is never a time of year that is not busy, but there are plenty of times when there are added pressures (e.g. academic work due in, school extra-curricular events, personal life events). Furthermore, primary school trainees are particularly good at finding things to do when they are not busy. However, by being aware of this you can start to plan when your personal peaks and troughs are. Make a plan to maximise the downtime, but also know that the 'crunch times' won't last for ever. The ability to keep plodding on, bit by bit, is a key skill.

The second most common issue for not thriving on placement is the feeling you are not being supported. If you are not sure what this support should look like, or what your/the school's role and responsibilities are, these are usually to be found within the paperwork you were given at the start of term. At the start of a course, this information can be overwhelming and of little immediate concern, yet later in the course it can be useful to revisit it. If you decide that there is an issue that needs to be resolved while on placement, in the first instance it is always best to speak directly to the school and try to work together to alleviate your concerns. You may wish to seek the advice of your university tutor too, as they are usually your second port of call in these situations. However, teachers and schools very much appreciate being informed of your concerns and the chance to work together on these in the first instance.

Finally, there is a small group who may consider that teaching is not for them. There can be a variety of reasons for this, but usually it is because their expectations of the profession do not match up to the reality. Often this can be around work–life balance, and it can be worth 'sticking it out' as it does often improve. The question of whether or not to leave a course should never be entered into lightly. You should take all available opportunities to speak to your central university careers services, your course leaders, your school, as well as family and friends. Depending on where you are in your teaching journey, having invested so much money in your training it can often be worth completing your course even if you have decided that teaching is not for you. This way you have the qualification in reserve for the future, and it would hold you in good stead for other jobs working with children. In some universities it is possible to 'drop' the QTS element of the course. This means that you could graduate with the academic modules but without the recommendation for qualified teacher status. Again, this could be useful in securing roles working with children in another capacity. For some people, however, they may well realise that teaching is not the career for them and they wish to leave immediately, and this too is OK. This brings an inevitable sense of disappointment (disappointment being the distance between your expectations and reality) but at least you explored this route. Had you not, you never would have known and may have lived your life thinking 'what if?'. If your mind is made up, do make sure that you again access to as many services and speak to as many people as possible to ensure you are aware of all of the possible routes that will be open to you in the future.

MENTAL HEALTH AND WELLBEING

SOCIAL MEDIA AND YOUR MENTAL HEALTH

Social media should come with one of the health warnings that appear on alcohol: taken in moderation and in the right circumstances it can be enjoyable, even positive. Social media can be a delightful platform for sharing teaching ideas, becoming inspired about lessons and providing support for teachers. However, it can also be an all-consuming, time-draining 'suck monster', which only shows students the sunny, happy, cheery mirages of other people's lives. It is easier for people to remember that social media should be consumed with care in 'normal life', but when completing a teacher training course you are in a slightly different, more vulnerable space. If you are on an undergraduate course it may seem like your friends have much fewer hours contact time, frequently miss lectures and go out all of the time. However, from day one of your course you are held to the same accountability levels as a professional teacher. If you are on one of the postgraduate routes into teaching, as you have to squash three years' worth of learning into a single year, you most likely do not even get a chance to see your family, let alone your friends. If you then factor in the general public opinion about primary school teaching – you play all day, finish at 3 p.m. and have all of the holidays – this all combines to mean that no one really understands the complexity of what you are doing (well, except for other trainee teachers and the teaching community – see communities of practice above).

If you are ever marking/planning on a Saturday night, one of the biggest mistakes you can make is looking on Facebook/Instagram at other people's lives. To quote Julia Roberts in *Pretty Woman*, 'Big mistake, huge'. Everyone, and I mean everyone, will be out travelling the world, out on rooftop bars with friends, or showing off their ripped bodies in the gym. You will be laminating, organising folders and reading about Piaget. However, imagine now the last 'Ahhhh, I gettit now, miss/sir' moment that you had with a child. You can imagine the scene. You're teaching Little Jonny (every class has a Little Jonny), and he looks blank. Really blank. He might actually be asleep, but his eyes are open, so you suspect he is still awake. You send the other children away to work independently and sit down to start the process of finding twelve new ways of explaining the same information you've just taught. You feel you are very much in for the long haul. Then you see a flicker on Jonny's face. It starts around the eyes and then spreads like soft butter to his lips. Finally, he mutters the words you have been longing to hear for what seems like days, 'Ahhh, I gettit now'. How did that moment make you feel? This is what you need to save. Usually, it is then ruined by a comically quizzical look from said child, as if to question, 'Well, why didn't you just explain it to me this way in the first place, what was with all the discussion?' Ignore the look, but hold onto that feeling.

On a Saturday evening, you may be in the trenches and slogging away, but you are plodding, working towards those moments. The moments when all thirty kids in your class are enthused, inspired and learning. When all thirty children in your class have their hands up, just waiting to share what they have thought about with you. Like anything worthwhile, those moments do not come for free, you have to graft. If you worked in a soulless cubicle, in an office, inputting data, or in telesales or organising some generic business then, yes, maybe you would have more free time to make your Instagram profile amazing. But you'd also miss out on those special moments. The 'Ahhh, I gettit now' moments, and the many, many, many like them. Please do not forget as you develop as a teacher, some things start to become a little more practised, and as with anything this then frees up a little time. You will never be completely free. However, it does get easier. The message of this section is to try to hold everything in perspective, which is hard when you are in the teaching trenches and you feel others are floating around. You too float, but *you also teach others to fly too* and you should not ever forget this, even if there are no pictures on rooftop bars of you doing this!

CASE STUDY 5.1   LGBTQ STUDENTS

Every year, LGBTQ students ask me if they can, or should, 'come out' in school. The fact that I am always asked this question illustrates the heteronormative world within which most of us still live. This section considers the options for LGBTQ students, as well as the law underpinning working in schools. For heterosexual students this section may serve to highlight some issues that your colleagues may face when working in schools. This is important, because you will be the workforce of the future. I would love to think that if everyone tried to walk a mile in someone else's shoes the world may be a more understanding place for everyone, rather than just the majority. It is important to note here that if you are comfortable to be your authentic self, whatever that might mean to you, you will be a happier more empowered individual. Happy people make happy teachers who enable their pupils to learn. If you have to self-censor, double guess yourself, and use time and energy to hide your identity this can be incredibly draining.

Let's start at the beginning. There is no requirement for anyone, irrespective of sexuality, to have to declare to whom they are attracted. However, if we take it as read that the world is indeed a heteronormative place, then assumptions are generally made by many that unless you particularly demonstrate difference from assumed 'gender roles' that you are in fact straight. So far, so clear. Where this becomes something to consider for LGBTQ students is usually in two places. The first is in the staff room with colleagues, when they are chatting about their weekend with their friends and family and the LGBTQ student wishes to join in. Some LGBTQ students feel comfortable revealing this aspect of their identity, and some do not. This can stem from negative personal past experiences or simply from being unsure of the staff's view (e.g. it could be a more traditional workforce or perhaps it is a religious school). Therefore, the first choice is not to mention anything at all. To keep all private and personal issues to themselves. Some heterosexual people also take this approach, although most people may find this completely shut-off approach a little difficult and isolating.

Some people may suggest engaging in staff-room conversations, but just changing the personal pronoun (e.g. from 'he' to 'she', or vice versa, or using 'they'). Of course, some folk feel happy with this swap

(Continued)

and this section is not trying to telling you the 'right way', as there are a variety of ways, but you have to find the one that suits you and your circumstances the best. Some people dislike this pronoun swap, as it does not feel authentic. It also presents issues with showing pictures or attending events.

Finally, there is revealing that you are LGBTQ in the staff room. You may wish to simply be yourself from day one, and when conversation turns to an aspect of your life, which reveals your sexuality, then you roll with it. After all, as Stonewall say, 'some people are gay/bi, get over it'. Or if you wish, you could speak to colleagues individually. Neither is right nor wrong. And there are of course a hundred variations of these scenarios in real life.

The second place that trainee teachers may wonder about presenting their authentic self is in the classroom with the children. Many teachers talk about their families with their pupils, and many of the children talk about their families with their teachers (some revealing a little bit more than they should at times). Teaching in school is a social activity, a community of learning. The children all come from different families, and personally I think it can only be a positive for the children to see different types of teachers. That said, you do not have to be an LGBTQ role model if you do not want to be. You get to choose. If you do decide to be authentic in the classroom then one way into this is to consider the books, posters and supporting materials in class. Are they representative of different families and different loves?

Many of the children in your class may not come from a traditional, nuclear family and extending the concept of family and love is a really great way to include all children. Audit the materials in your classroom and see if you need to consider updating these. Then, when teaching and at an appropriate moment, if it comes up, you can simply respond how you would normally to the children. Be prepared for them to question you, thinking you might have made a mistake, e.g. 'you can't have a wife silly, you're a Mrs. Don't you mean husband?' To which you can simply explain, 'No, I do mean wife as I have a wife. Boys can have a wife or a husband, and girls can choose too. You can of course choose to have neither!'

Sometimes, the trainees with whom I work ask the question, 'Aren't children too young to know about these things?', which I find quite an interesting idea. So let us be clear here. You are not going to talk to the children about gay sex, in fact you're not going to be talking to the children about sex. In conclusion, no one is talking to the children about any kind of sex. What you are going to do, however, is talk about love: when a man and a man love each other, or when a woman and a woman love each other, or when a man and woman love each other: simple. There are much scarier things for kids to be worrying about than who loves who. Some children's books I have used in schools have reduced me to tears over the years, and some still haunt me to this day. For example: Exhibit A: During a famine, stepmother decides to abandon children in a wood, so they do not all starve to death. The children end up kidnapped by a cannibalistic witch but they outsmart her and kill her and run off with her riches (*Hansel and Gretel*). Exhibit B: An abused child is evacuated to live with an illiterate old man whose wife and child have died. After successfully integrating, the boy is returned to his abusive, mentally ill mother, who locks him in a cupboard with his new baby sister. By the time the old man tracks the boy down the baby, which the young boy is holding locked in the cupboard with him, is dead and the child is traumatised (*Goodnight Mister Tom*). Exhibit C: A young girl watches as the streets of her small German town fill with soldiers who round up some of the citizens. She follows the truck into the forest where she finds a concentration camp. She starts to bring the children food, but then she and the children 'disappear' (*Rose Blanche*). Different relationships are all based on love, and there is nothing scary about that. Audit your curriculum and the resources that you use. Consider whether these are representative of the wider world. Do they only show white, heterosexual, able-bodied mums and dads with two children?

The third aspect that trainee teachers sometimes wonder about is how parents will react, particularly if the school in which they are working is of a religious nature. It is important to note that no religion promotes hatred or intolerance as their core belief. Individuals do differ on their views of the world (e.g. dietary preferences), and yet quite often, contrary to what is sometimes published in the press, diverse communities manage to live in harmony. Holding a belief is very different from imposing your views on others. It may be helpful to consider, at this point, what the law says. The law has moved on from Section 28 (Local Government Act, 1988), which prohibited the teaching of homosexuality in schools. All schools now operate under the Equality Act 2010, which brought together the Sex Discrimination

(Continued)

Act 1975, Race Relations Act 1976 and the Disability Discrimination Act 1995. The Equality Act 2010 offers protection to all against all forms of discrimination, including homophobia. What might this look like in practice? Well, it would mean that if teachers in your school talk about their different sex partners then you as an LGBTQ student would also be able to. It means that a school would not be able to treat you and a heterosexual student teacher differently. That said, sadly sometimes LGBTQ people are still discriminated against, and it is the duty of all of us, if we see this, to challenge it. However, understanding how the law can protect you, while not a magic wand, certainly helps.

Finally, what can we all do to help to create an inclusive environment in your school, for everyone irrespective of sexuality? One of the key skills to develop is the ability to ask questions, rather than make assumptions. This works well in a variety of contexts. The next time you are unsure of something, just ask. Obviously, not in a scary 'in your face' sort of a way, but with a more nuanced approach, 'I noticed that you said you X, or I was really interested when you said you Y – could you tell me a bit more about that?' If you hear the term 'gay' being used incorrectly or other homophobic language being used in a school by staff or pupils, challenging this is the first step. This can be as simple as repeating back to them what you heard and questioning it. If you do not feel comfortable in the moment, do make sure that you report it to the senior leadership team at a later date.

There are a number of LGBTQ and school support resources, but included below are three that you might like to start with, which are described in their own words:

Stonewall: Stonewall 'works with institutions to create inclusive and accepting cultures, to ensure institutions understand and value the huge benefits brought to them'. More specifically regarding schools, they 'deliver training, produce resources and develop membership programmes to empower teachers and education professionals to tackle homophobia, biphobia and transphobia in schools and colleges' (Stonewall, 2019). They also have an Education Team who can offer bespoke support for schools and teachers.

Inclusion for All: 'Inclusion for All is an umbrella term for a series of training strategies developed and piloted by Shaun Dellenty alongside serving teachers [and] education professionals that aim to foster positive LGBT+ inclusion in schools and communities, thus aiming to significantly reduce incidents of prejudice related bullying and language' (Inclusion for All, 2019).

Naz and Matt Foundation: 'Naz and Matt Foundation exists to empower and support LGBTQI (Lesbian, Gay, Bisexual, Transgender, Queer, Questioning, and Intersex) individuals, their friends and family to work towards resolving challenges linked to sexuality or gender identity, particularly where religion is heavily influencing the situation' (Naz and Matt Foundation, 2019). They are a registered UK charity and have won multiple awards for their work building bridges between religious and LGBTQI+ communities. They provide support and links to further resources for LGBTQ individuals including legal advice and forum support.

CHAPTER SUMMARY

- University and training sessions are so much more than PowerPoints and notes – they are interactive.
- Discussions, interactions and questions *are* learning.
- No one will understand what you are going through like your teacher training friends. So do invest time developing a network of support when on campus.
- If you like your mentor, that's great. If not you should listen to what they say anyway, as you both have the common goal of the pupils' best interests at heart.
- Have I mentioned getting organised?!
- Be aware of how social media can influence and make you feel. Learn to be more than your phone. Be a real person, in your real life: be present.

FURTHER READING

Kokkinos, C. M. (2011) 'Job stressors, personality and burnout in primary school teachers', *British Journal of Educational Psychology*, 77(1): 229–243.

This article is a good exploration of the association between burnout, personality characteristics and job stressors in primary school teachers. This study was set in Cyprus but has links to teaching in England.

Cockburn, A. and Handscomb, G. (eds) (2012) *Teaching Children 3–11*, 3rd edition. London: Sage.

This book has many great sections of interest for the trainee teacher. Of particular relevance is the chapter called 'How am I doing?' by Ann Oliver, which looks to help you gain an insight into your own teaching by considering what successful teaching looks like and how to improve.

Sellars, M. (2014) *Reflective Practice for Teachers*, 2nd edition. London: Sage.

This book offers a great insight into a variety of really practical application topics such as emotional intelligence or understanding the learning process. However, the chapter I would like to draw your attention to is on the 'Importance of positive thinking', which is as good for you as it is for your pupils.

6

SAVVY ONLINE RESEARCH, CROSS-CURRICULAR PLANNING AND DIVERSITY IN SCHOOLS

This
CHAPTER
EXPLORES:

- the online offerings available to you and why you should join the Chartered College of Teaching
- what you want your pupils to learn, how and why, before you start cross-curricular planning
- different issues of diversity faced by teachers and pupils.

ACADEMIC

ONLINE OFFERINGS

When learning how to teach there are a variety of university lectures and seminars to attend as well as mentoring and coaching in school and attending school training sessions. In addition, you are also expected to develop your knowledge through reading.

On the reading front, there is some good news. These days you do not even need to leave your house (provided you have a reliable Internet connection) to access reading material, and it has never been easier to find reading resources. However, there is a real skill in developing your critical literacy about what is appropriate to read, and how to find this information in a strategic, time sensitive manner. This section looks at making the most of the online offering, with a view to saving you time while also developing your knowledge. It considers your university online support, Google books and a range of research-informed sources of information that might be worth exploring first.

YOUR UNIVERSITY ONLINE OFFERING

In this section, we are going to start small and then go big. As such, the best place to start is your module/course handbook or guide. These often have recommended readings in them, and these lists are usually reviewed each year as the new academic planning is done. These lists will be tailored to your particular course and your specific essays, and are in the first instance the best place to start. While you are reading your module handbook, do cast your eye over the learning outcomes for your module, this will orientate you about what each particular module is focused on. I am constantly amazed by how few students actually read and consider these documents. I suspect that they are given out at a time when students' attention is on other things, e.g. assignment dates. However, they really are one of the most important documents to read on your course. Of course, some poor soul has slaved away over the summer months to create them for you, so do read them repeatedly throughout your course, as you will be able to gain different perspectives on your reading at different times.

The second place that students sometimes overlook is the VLE (Blackboard, Canvas, Moodle, etc.) that their provider uses. Some lecturers will upload key readings or parts of articles to such a platform, but many will simply reference their source within their lecture notes or PowerPoint. Therefore, when you are searching for information on a topic, it can be useful to open the resources from sessions and look at the references. Then you can search for these readings to start with, before considering who these authors/researchers have been reading. Again, this is an often overlooked resource. Yes, of course it does require you to log on and click through slides, but generally the resources that are on these sites are some of the most key. So it is worth your time exploring these, even if you do not understand the relevance initially, allow yourself to be guided by an experienced practitioner (e.g. your lecturer). As a general rule of thumb, if your lecturer has gone to the trouble of creating or uploading something, you can almost guarantee that this information is important.

Many institutions have been growing and developing their online resources enabling learners to access materials at a time and place that suits them. For most online libraries, you can search through databases as well as through the basic university catalogue. Some of the databases you may wish to start with when researching education topics are: Taylor & Francis; ScienceDirect; British Education Index; Emerald (for educational management); and Education Research Complete. However, alternatively, there can be other approaches, which have recently been developed. These alternative literature search pathways are provided by your library; a good example of one of these is BrowZine (an app and a website), which enables you to go in and search for journals through gradually narrowing topics before browsing the titles. The only word of caution to be noted for this approach is that many of these search function have originated in the USA. As such you will find the educational terms used (and education can be located within the Social Sciences tab on BrowZine) are American, and as such K–12 (kindergarten to 12th grade) will correlate to the titles you are looking for. Once you find what you are looking for you can save your articles and journals to your BrowZine shelf.

If database searches and browsing for journal titles is not the way you would like to approach your learning you can always conduct a key-word search through search engines such as Discover. This search provider enables you, in one search, to explore books and e-books, journal articles, theses, even digital media. However, a key-word search will only ever be as good as the words you search. Obviously the broader the term searched, the broader the results that are yielded. You can filter these results with the various tabs, which are located down the side of the page, or you can simply search for terms that are more specific. Be aware that when looking in international journals the terms that you might use may be different from those used globally. Furthermore, it can really be useful to arrange a quick tutorial with a librarian to learn how to use truncated searches. Truncated searches are also known as 'wildcard searching'. This means you can search for a key word or term as well as the variant spellings of that term. The most common way to truncate when searching is to remove the ending of the word and add an asterisk (*).

If you are researching a particularly niche area or a topic which has only just come to the fore, you may find that there is not much literature available. In this case, if you manage to find one article or book then it can be useful to read the references of this piece of literature. Then you can set about gathering and reading those sources and again for each one consider what the author(s) have also been reading. You may find that this method takes you back in time to 'older' sources rather than bringing your forward to the more contemporary literature, so do bear this in mind. However, it can be useful in terms of providing additional search terms and sub-issues to consider. You can always then do a key search for the authors you have found, and see if they have updated their research or added to it later.

Finally, if you are really stuck it can be very useful to leave the house and go to the library. Imagine that. Librarians are the unsung heroes of universities everywhere. Make an appointment to speak with one or see if they are running any classes on common topics/issues on campus. Then explain what you are struggling with and watch them do their magic.

OTHER ONLINE RESOURCES

There is a plethora of online resources available to student teachers; some are more research informed than others. Therefore, in a bid to save busy teachers time, we are going to consider a selection of the most useful and try to outline the key features, which make them so helpful. Obviously, by its very nature, the online offering is constantly evolving and so think of this list as the highlights rather than an exhaustive list.

First is the Education Endowment Foundation (EEF) created in 2011, a charity designed to promote educational attainment for all children, especially those from low-income families. The EEF identifies and trials educational innovations, which can promote educational achievement for disadvantaged children. To date the EEF has 'allocated £57 million to over 100 evaluations and projects, involving 4,900 schools and 620,000 pupils' (EFF, 2015). One of the most useful features on their website is the Sutton Trust EEF Teaching and Learning Toolkit. This at a glance table allows educational professionals to assess the cost, impact and evidence strength of a variety of interventions. If there is an intervention that you would like further information about there is the option to click into the section and more detail is provided, including 'what should I consider?' and the 'technical appendix', which includes the references used and abstracts which can be very useful when looking for readings on a particular topic. It also considers how much it would cost to implement an intervention, which is of critical importance these days for schools operating on tight budgets.

Next is the Chartered College of Teaching, which offers free membership for trainee teachers. The College is a recognised professional body for the teaching profession and it intends to augment the status and quality of teaching through supporting teachers. It aims to do this by connecting the profession, informing the profession and inspiring the profession. Benefits of joining include being able to use the College's education and research database, access to the Chartered College events and discounted entrance to the College's conferences. However, by far the best tool is the members' only 'My College' platform. This online space is an attractive, easy to navigate, veritable joy of research and teaching-related information, which is presented in such an accessible manner that it is a pleasure to access.

Journals, books and websites all require the trainee teacher to have enough time, space and quiet to be able to read, and sometimes this can be a little tricky to navigate. Therefore, another good addition to the trainee teacher toolkit is podcasts. If you download podcasts to your phone, you can then listen to them when out walking the dog, travelling to school or even just doing the housework of an evening. However, you are able to do other things while also listening to podcasts. BBC Radio 4 has a great series that is still live called *The Educators*, which covers a variety of topics.

Another podcast series, 'Intelligence: Born Smart, Born Equal and Born Different', is not a comfortable listen, as it calls into question deep-held beliefs about intelligence and the role of education. That said, it is a brilliantly thought-provoking series which really ensures that you develop and redefine your own teaching philosophy. Reasonably new to the podcast scene is 'Parentland', which as you can gather from the title is aimed at parents. However, there is much overlap and background information and research, which is useful for a teacher to understand. In the show a journalist and scientist take a research-informed journey into common topics and unpick these 'common ideas' using experts from the field and research. Finally, another recommended podcast would be 'Four Thought'. These short talks are on a variety of topics, personal to the speaker. While not specifically on education, the podcasts might inform you about a topic that affects the lives of the pupils you teach, might educate you about a topic you should be teaching in school or might simply make you a better-informed human about the perspectives of different people. My standout favourite is by Matthew Syed who discusses 'does talent trump effort?' I was struck when listening to this podcast for the first time about the practical application of ideas into my classroom and how to engage learners in their own development. Podcast offerings are updated quite frequently, and so it can be worth subscribing to a podcast feed to keep up to date. There are many podcast shows, which you might like to subscribe to including Ted Talks Education, TES: The Education Podcast, or The Cult of Pedagogy Podcast, but you will quickly find your own favourites.

PLACEMENT

CROSS-CURRICULAR PLANNING

When you embark on your teacher education, you tend to observe lessons, teach small groups, and concentrate on the core subject and then move wider. As the year progresses, you will develop the skills to plan individual lessons, series of lessons and then unit plans. However, a common issue for trainee teachers is cross-curricular planning. Usually, this is because students are not aware of the ultimate aim of their cross-curricular planning and/or they do not have the subject/pedagogical knowledge to deliver each subject without 'watering it down' (DES, 1992). Therefore, this section highlights that there are different ways in which, according to Barnes (2015), you can plan cross-curricular units of work. It is important that you know, to start with, that Barnes identified seven different approaches to cross-curricular planning: tokenistic, hierarchical, single transferrable subject, multi-disciplinary, inter-disciplinary, opportunistic, double focus. Each one of these approaches has a different aim and approach. Do not assume that simply 'making links' in one lesson to another lesson is the full scope of 'doing cross-curricular learning' as this would be cheating both you and your pupils of the full range and depth that cross-curricular learning can offer.

Once you have a clear road map of where you are heading to and why, the next stop is for you to access both the National Curriculum and your school's planning. The National Curriculum outlines the programme of study that you should deliver for your year group (core subjects) or key stage (foundation subjects). As well as reading the programmes of study, do make sure to consider the 'purpose of study' as well as the 'aims' of the subject because there can be really useful insights in these small introduction paragraphs, which you may otherwise miss. However, while the current version of the National Curriculum (2013) does indeed provide teachers with planning 'freedoms', it is not entirely helpful for new teachers setting out. The teaching and learning of the core subjects of English, maths and science are given much more detail than the foundation subjects. This is not surprising given that these subjects form part of the statutory reporting for schools. However, the weighting of core subjects versus foundation subjects is really part of a larger debate. It is worth noting that this 'two-tier' (and it may be argued 'three-tier' with the third tier now being the subjects that are 'outsourced', e.g. foreign languages, music, computing and PE) curriculum is nothing new (Hadlow Report, 1926). However, well-planned cross-curricular units are an approach that can help to ameliorate this situation. But what does this all mean for you? Well, it means that you should try to access your school's previous/current plans to enable you to see the National Curriculum in context, and plan for coherence and progression across the units, terms and years.

Your school's long-term and medium-term planning (which usually can be accessed on the school intranet, but do seek permission first from your mentor) will show you how subjects/themes and learning are mapped across the school. It will also show you what your class will have previously learned (but do check with their previous class teacher because as with all things in a school they are very much subject to change). It is at this point it would be useful to speak to your class teacher or mentor in school and discuss the ideas you have had and the type of cross-curricular approach you wish to take. When you look at these units, consider what the outcome of the unit was and then work forwards/backwards across the lessons to understand how the learning progressed. Sometimes, it is not clear how a teacher will have taken the end of key stage learning and created a unit of work. A good example is the history curriculum for Key Stage 2, which states, 'children should be taught about ... a local history study' (DfE, 2013). So you need to have knowledge of several factors to even begin to consider planning this unit. For example, in Key Stage 1, when learning about 'significant historical events, people and places in their own locality' (DfE, 2013), what did the children learn? Can you build on this prior learning, but not repeat learning? As learning about local history covers the entire Key Stage 2, what are the teachers above and below you planning and how does your unit fit? By accessing the school's plans you can see how your unit fits into the much wider school learning. This is important as it will minimise repetition, and can ensure relevance and coherence for children on their educational journeys.

When you are actually planning the units of work you need to ensure that your pupils make progress, in line with the identified outcomes of your approach (see Barnes, 2015). This can be achieved by ensuring that the skills and knowledge that you are planning correspond carefully with the subjects that you are delivering. Each subject has its own pedagogy (think teaching approach). For example, a common 'trap to avoid' is the English and history combination. It is altogether too easy to feel that you are teaching your class about English and history – but when you look more closely at the learning and the outcomes these are all in fact English based. Another more illustrative example is PE pedagogy. You simply would not dream of creating a PowerPoint of how to do a forward roll, present it to the children and then ask them to write about it. You would, instead, model skills, breaking it down into component parts, then allow the children some controlled practice, giving formative feedback, maybe some peer feedback. Then you might chain the moves together and allow some free practice by the end, perhaps looking for good examples to show others. This is because the sequence, as outlined above, is specific to the teaching of PE. Quite often confused teaching delivery and teaching of the 'wrong'/unintended subject happens when trainees are not very familiar with that subject. Therefore, another useful source of support to consider is the subject leader in school who will be able to advise you about specific subject pedagogies to deliver subject-specific outcomes in learning. Many subjects also have their own organisations, which you can join online.

OUTSIDE PROVIDERS AND CROSS-CURRICULAR PLANNING

Many schools employ a variety of outside providers to deliver certain curriculum subjects for the school while teachers have their PPA time. Not always but very commonly the subjects that the outside providers deliver are foreign languages, music, PE and sometimes computing. This may have a variety of implications for a trainee teacher. It may mean that you do not normally have the opportunity to observe these sessions as you are on your PPA time with the teacher. Furthermore, as these subjects are delivered by the outside provider it may mean that you do not have the opportunity to deliver these subjects yourself. One possibility to ensure that you do have the opportunity to teach right across the curriculum is to use cross-curricular planning. Fortunately, many of the subjects listed above lend themselves particularly well to being integrated across the curriculum. It is also important that pupils in your class see teachers delivering all subjects as they may start to make unhelpful associations about the importance and/or difficulty of these subjects if they are always delivered by an outside provider. For example, they may feel that foreign-language learning is just too hard and that is why sir does not deliver it or they may start to feel that PE is not as important as other subjects are, which is why miss does not teach it. Integrating all subjects, even if you do not opt for a double-focus approach (Barnes, 2015), creates a more broad and balanced curriculum, helping all children to reach their potential. Should the teaching of some of these subjects fill you with fear, this is your opportunity to model for your pupils how to learn, particularly when something is 'difficult'. Pupils can often feel that teachers know everything, and that they do not have to work or practise.

The first step to include subjects which are taught by outside providers into your planning is to understand what they previously learned in the subject and what they are going to be learning. Sometimes access to outside providers can be tricky to negotiate as many of these teachers work in multiple settings, and as such are travelling from one place to another. It can be useful to let them know what you are planning to do and why, and to try to arrange a mutually beneficial time to discuss this with them. Once you have discovered prior and intended learning you may wish to ask the outside provider for recommendations for materials, or pedagogical resources, as they will have a full repertoire of these supports. You could also offer to share your cross-curricular planning with the specialist; in this way they too could then reference the learning you are doing with their own, helping to create a coherent curriculum approach. They may also (but this is not to be expected) check that you are along the 'right lines' with your planning.

MENTAL HEALTH AND WELLBEING

ISSUES OF DIVERSITY

Issues of diversity in the classroom can be a two-way street. They may stem from the teacher or come from the pupils/their families. In this section, we will look at issues teachers may face personally before moving on to consider the same topic from the pupils' perspectives. However, before we get started, let us set the scene. Diversity is not something that only concerns others, you know the 'diverse'; like the 'vegans', the 'anxious', the 'gays', the 'foreigners' or the 'disabled', for example. We are all diverse in a multitude of ways and this is normal. All people should be treated equally, but that does not mean in the same way, as no two people are the same. Teachers in particular should look to 'normalise' the concept of diversity; it is not something you need to shy away from (despite what some tabloid newspapers may tell you), as it is just normal life. And neither do you have to tie yourselves up in knots in case you offend someone. Chances are, with your friends and family, as these are named individuals who you know well, you ask considered questions, do not make assumptions and when appropriate ask them how they would like to be supported. After all, isn't that what you would want? If you want to understand diversity, you should seek to understand humans.

ISSUES OF DIVERSITY: TEACHERS

Teachers are real life human beings and not automatons or robots. As such each teacher brings with them their unique attributes and ability to inspire pupils in different ways. Some teachers are avid sportspeople, while others prefer arts and crafts. Some teachers enjoy sharing about their pets while other teachers like talking to their pupils about cooking. You are, of course, under no obligation to share anything with your pupils, however, you may find this a little difficult and also the type of personality generally attracted to teaching usually enjoys these types of discussions with children.

These discussions about life outside school can be important for a number of reasons. They help to address the power imbalance, where children share about their lives but do not know anything about their teachers. By talking to the children, you also become a much more 'real' individual rather than just a 'teacher'. However, it is important when entering into conversations with pupils that you uphold Part Two of the Teachers' Standards (DfE, 2011) and are aware of your legal obligations outlined in *School Teachers' Pay and Conditions* (DfE, 2018). Reading these two documents will help to keep both you and the children whom you teach safe.

As no two teachers are the same, this also means that each teacher has different beliefs and ways in which they choose to live their lives. This may mean that some teachers feel more comfortable than others in being their 'authentic' self, maybe for reasons concerning LGBTQ (see Chapter 5), religion, disability, gender or culture. However, being able to be your 'authentic' self is important because it helps to make you feel included, and fosters a sense of belonging (Maslow, 1943). It may be useful to know that the Equality Act (2010) now replaces all previous legislation in this area and ensures that you cannot be discriminated against for whatever your protected characteristics are and these may overlap.

Some issues of diversity are visible while others may not be and again it is the choice of the individual whether or not they choose to disclose. For example, some teachers may feel comfortable to reveal, in schools, that they are dyslexic and, as such, they have discussed strategies (researching spellings before lessons, modelling looking up words for students, using computer software to generate text, not being asked to take meeting notes, etc.). In addition, some teachers may not feel safe enough to want to reveal their disability.

ISSUES OF DIVERSITY: PUPILS

The wonderful thing about Tigger is that there is only one. That is the same delightful thing about children, each one is unique. Ideally, in your classroom, you are trying to cultivate an environment where everyone is comfortable being different, but all your pupils know that they are equal, respected and safe. It is you as a teacher who creates and manages this atmosphere. Moreover, one of the best ways in which you can do this is by learning to ask questions and giving your pupils the space and time to talk about themselves. Learning to ask questions simply cannot be underestimated as a key life skill for you and the pupils you teach. A well-considered, respectful question has the power to educate (both the person asking, and those listening to the answer, as well as sometimes providing a space for them to reflect) and also helps to create an inclusive environment. All too often, while well meaning, people can try to remove difference and promote a vision of 'we're all the same', but we are not all the same really, and that is perfectly OK and should be celebrated.

Show and tell is a great vehicle for allowing children to share with their class what is important to them in their family, it is also good for developing speaking and listening in a non-formal setting. In one school with which I worked, they had developed in the EYFS provision something that they called 'culture bags'. Each week a different child took the bag home and filled it with items relating to their culture and brought it back to share with the class. Some children brought in religious dress and sacred texts, others brought in football match ticket stubs and pie receipts while other children brought in pictures of going out on a Sunday walk – the key message being that everyone has a culture, whether it is going to the temple, or going to the football or simply having a walk. Whatever it is that you do with your family which is important to you is important and valued. In multicultural classes, the sharing of ideas and knowledge happens quite organically and children, being naturally curious, are best placed to learn from each other. In mono-cultural settings, irrespective of culture, it can be more difficult to authentically share ideas, as there is little diversity between pupils. Therefore, care should be taken to plan this into the curriculum using guest speakers, books, resources, online materials or partnership schools (both within UK and abroad). Attention should be paid, however, not to introduce these aspects into the curriculum in a tokenistic manner, or what Kramsch (1991) calls 'the culture of the four Fs: foods, fairs, folklore, and statistical facts'. You may also like to be mindful of representations of people and whether these reinforce stereotypes or help to challenge them. A good example of this is the well-meaning British Values displays, which tend to feature predominately white, heterosexual males, or the French displays, which usually have a man in a stripy top, a baguette under his arm, and onions around his neck pushing a bicycle. When a pupil of mine returned to Pakistan for Eid one year, I asked him to keep a video diary. When he returned to school we all watched his travels over a series of days. The other pupils simply could not believe that the boy that was sat next to them was the same boy who had been zipping through the fields on the back of a scooter just moments before. However, it was the more mundane aspects of the diary which provided the most inroads into learning, such as meal times, shopping and visiting grandparents, all elements of daily life that the pupils could relate to and explore. This contextualisation of life in Pakistan was particularly important at that time, because Pakistan was being regularly featured in news outlets and the media with negative connotations. As the news and social media present increasingly diametrically opposed views (for or against, in or out, leave or remain, yes or no, best thing since sliced bread or simply the worst idea known to people) it is the role of the teacher to provide more nuance for pupils, to enable them to question representations of nations and peoples for themselves, to find the 'grey areas', explore these and to be happy to understand both sides of an argument. However, they need to be provided with alternative perspectives and the time and safe space to talk about these issues (as well as being enabled to talk about them in a sensitive manner). The Philosophy for Children approach is a great vehicle to deliver this for children.

What exactly does creating safe spaces mean and how do they help to keep children safe? A safe space means that pupils' needs are met and they feel comfortable talking about what is important to them. For instance, if a respected and valued climate is fostered, this then enables children to feel safe as they are able to talk about whatever is bothering them or simply whatever they want to without fear of being judged, shouted at or bullied. This climate is incredibly important for you as a teacher to create in your classroom, and simply cannot be underestimated. This is because it is part of your safeguarding duty to be 'particularly alert to the potential need for early help for a child who: is disabled and has specific additional needs; has special educational needs (whether or not they have a statutory Education, Health and Care Plan); is a young carer; is showing signs of being drawn in to anti-social or criminal behaviour, including gang involvement and association with organised crime groups; is frequently missing/goes missing from care or from home; is at risk of modern slavery, trafficking or exploitation; is at risk of being radicalised or exploited; is in a family circumstance presenting challenges for the child, such as drug and alcohol misuse, adult mental health issues and domestic abuse; is misusing drugs or alcohol themselves' (DfE, 2019: 7). Sometimes pupils come into school with a clear and correct personal history. However, many pupils experience situations such as being young carers or frequently going hungry and no one is aware of these situations. All too often pupils may feel that if they are experiencing these issues it is somehow 'their fault' or a source of shame. Shame is a powerful tool that operates on how an individual feels about themselves, with the feeling that in some way they have done something wrong. There is a brilliant episode of *The Digital Human* podcast entitled 'Shame', which really unpicks this emotion further. However, by creating a safe space to talk to you and in your classroom, you help to keep children safe, as they will be able to talk to you about issues that matter to them.

It is at this point that the difference between a difficult conversation (e.g. a sensitive topic) and a safeguarding issue (e.g. a pupil revealing that they may be being groomed) should be noted. In the instance where you feel it is a safeguarding issue, you should not investigate the issue yourself, nor should you promise the child not to tell anyone else. You should instead report your concerns directly to the safeguarding lead in your school and follow your school's safeguarding policy. All trainee teachers and teachers should be familiar with the school's safeguarding policy before starting work/placement; however, if this section is making you wonder about your school's particular policy then you need to make sure that you access this policy and read it with immediate effect. However, it is certainly worth flagging up with you that in the case of issues of safeguarding you do have a very clear and defined role. According to *Keeping Children Safe in Education* (DfE, 2019: 5), this duty is defined as 'protecting children from maltreatment; preventing impairment of children's health or development; ensuring that children grow up in circumstances consistent with the provision of safe and effective care; taking action to enable all children to have the best outcomes'.

If the topic is not a safeguarding issue, but is something that could potentially be a difficult conversation, it can be quite tricky at first for a trainee teacher not to panic when pupils enter into this type of conversation with you. Student teachers have to be able to develop a series of strategies for dealing with unexpected and possibly difficult topics of conversation. As there is often no 'right' answer it is useful to consider the following scenarios and what you would do. If you are unsure, these would be useful topics to discuss at school with your mentors or to take to a seminar for discussion:

- A pupil asks you if there is a God.
- A pupil makes a stereotypical statement about a group of people, e.g. 'All X do Y', or 'My dad says, "all X are Y"'.
- Two pupils are engaged in an argument about what are boy jobs and what are girl jobs.
- Pupils start to question you about something that they have seen on the news related to drugs.
- A pupils tells you they cannot sleep because they are so worried about the upcoming SATs.

It is important that all children have the opportunity to explore their beliefs and that all beliefs (provided that they are not contravening fundamental British Values or the law) should be respected. Your job as the teacher is to facilitate these discussions and ensure that everyone has a voice. You may also act as a researcher, if the situation is appropriate, modelling for the children how they might seek out answers to questions that they wish to explore when they are on their own. You may wish to model questioning the sources that you retrieve from the Internet and to look at reliable and trustworthy sources of information for children. And sometimes you might say, 'you know what [insert curious child's name here], that is a *really* interesting question. I have no idea, let's research this together and learn about it as a class.' This is a very powerful model, through which you can question sources, compare viewpoints and look at learning together.

CASE STUDY 6.1   THE BUSY WORKING PARENT

Each year a number of BWPs (busy working parents) enrol on teacher education courses. Each year the BWPs are usually worried about their ability to manage a home life, university work and placement while simultaneously ensuring that their children are still fed and clothed and the mortgage is paid. And each year, I am never worried about BWPs. I now know that the BWPs have a time-management super power, which enables them to be ruthlessly efficient, organised and focused, meaning that they are able to organise their workload and still have time for a family life. I am not saying that this is in any way easy. Far from it, the pitfall, which the BWP tends to fall into, is not looking after themselves as much as they should do. Therefore, the aim of this section is to highlight for any BWPs that you should not worry so much. The sole fact that you are indeed worrying illustrates that you are aware of the magnitude of what you are trying to accomplish and you are ready to take steps to address the challenges. Secondly, this section aims to provide the BWPs (and any other time poor trainee teachers) with some practical tips for becoming a teacher while also trying to find five minutes to yourself, to look after you. After all, if you 'go down' everything else goes down with you – so it is so important to practise a little self-care. This is because neglecting self-care is the common 'fault' with BWPs. They are tremendous at looking after their fellow students, their children and their parents, but rubbish at looking after themselves to the same standards.

(Continued)

Let us now look at some practical tips for BWPs:

1   At the start of your course or when you receive your assignments
    have a journal blast. This means spend one day locating journal
    articles that you might need. You may need to add to this collection
    as you progress, but as soon as you receive your essay, you should
    locate your journals. Then print physical copies. Then, every time
    you leave the house, you pop one or two journal articles into your
    bag. So if you are taking the kids to swimming class, or you are
    doing the after school pick up or maybe just a drop off at football
    and you have a spare five minutes, you can start reading. Have a
    pack of post-it notes and an envelope handy too – you are going
    to write on the post-its all the key ideas that come to mind while
    reading and then drop these into the envelope (see Chapter 3 for
    reading ideas).
2   As a BWP, you probably do this already but have a timeline to deliver
    essays or projects on time and work backwards. Put this in the
    kitchen so all can see and all can support you.
3   Also in the kitchen, provided your family are old enough, allocate jobs to
    individuals. BWPs tend to do everything themselves as 'it's just easier'.
    Yes, it is in the first instance, until your family 'are trained'. But seri-
    ously, consider all your jobs such as loading dishwasher, or putting on
    a load of washing or walking the dog – do all of these tasks have to be
    done by you? I know what you are now thinking, but they won't do as
    good a job as me, and you are probably right, but for the year(s) that you
    are training does this matter too much? You need to make time for you,
    and while training things will have to change. And let's face it, while
    they might not do as good a job as you, they have to start somewhere
    and it's better than no job being done, which is what will happen if you
    'go down'. Once you start to 'loosen control' you never know, you might
    quite like it!
4   Make sure you speak to wider family members about what you have
    to do and when. In addition, do not expect them to complexly under-
    stand at first because in their minds you are a) a student and b) just
    playing with kids and finishing at 3.30 p.m. Be prepared to do some
    educating. Rope in grandparents, aunties, uncles and the neighbour-
    hood babysitting circle.
5   It is OK to be a little selfish during your teacher training. However,
    you need to prioritise you and your needs. This is not because you

are a self-indulgent monster, but because if you do not look after yourself and make some time to see your friends or exercise you will not be able to take care of everyone.

6   When essay writing, gather all the post-it notes you have in your envelope and separate these into similar themes. These will then become the paragraphs in your essay.

7   Batch cook everything over the weekend and then freeze in labelled containers. Tempting as it is to not to bother with the labels, these are key, as no one enjoys dinner roulette.

8   Make sure that you give your jobs specific time allocations. This is because 'planning' can easily take up an entire Sunday. By giving this task a specific time, it ensures you remain focused. A good way to ensure this is by planning in 'something nice' with your family for after you have finished. This really helps to focus the mind.

9   And finally, you need to know you're doing an amazing job. Your house might not be as tidy as you would like, and maybe your essay didn't get the mark that you wanted, and you feel incredibly guilty about the amount of time you spend with your children – but this isn't for ever and for the moment *you are amazing* as you're doing it all. Now, print out the sentence 'you're amazing' and stick it to your forehead until it sinks in.

CHAPTER SUMMARY

- Spend a whole day or two exploring online offerings. This will save you time in the long run.
- Online offerings are much, much more than just Google Books.
- Join the Chartered College of Teaching.
- Before rushing into cross-curricular planning consider not only what you want your pupils to learn, but how and why.
- Get even more organised!
- You are not a robot so do be aware of your own unconscious bias.

FURTHER READING

Barnes, J. (2015) *Cross-curricular Learning 3–14*, 3rd edition. London: Sage.

This is a great starting place for cross-curricular planning, considering the why and how you plan to deliver the curriculum.

Knowles, G. and Holmstrom, R. (2013) *Understanding Family Diversity and Home–School Relations*. Abingdon: Routledge.

A slight degree of overlap with the text that follows; however, this book focuses more on the family dynamic. It includes chapters on mixed-race families, gay and lesbian families, families living in poverty and bereavement in families.

Knowles, G. and Lander, V. (2011) *Diversity, Equality and Achievement in Education*. London: Sage.

A fantastic book, which considers diversity in all its varied forms, for example: class, gender, race and disability. A great foundation book for all teachers.

7

APPLYING FOR JOBS, NAVIGATING PARENTS' EVENING AND DEALING WITH WORRIES

This CHAPTER EXPLORES:

- applying for jobs and how to find the option that works for you, from being a supply teacher to working abroad
- how to handle parents' evening and make the most of it
- dealing with your own worries and how to deal with them in a way that does not take over your life.

ACADEMIC

APPLYING FOR JOBS

Applying for jobs can be stressful on top of everything else that a trainee teacher has to do in a normal week. Therefore, controversially, this chapter opens with a question: do you really want to apply for a full-time position now? Your reaction to this question is most likely to be positioned somewhere between 'Of course, I have a huge intrinsic drive to inspire, motivate and positively impact pupils' learning' and 'Yes, I'm broke, I need a full-time, permanent job'. Both responses are perfectly valid. However, the first part of this section is going to explore 'going on supply'. It is the opener to this chapter, as it does not get the credit it deserves; it is often regarded as the poor substitute for obtaining that coveted full-time permanent position. This is not true; there are a number of benefits that supply teaching has to offer, and they deserve to be taken seriously and considered.

SUPPLY TEACHING

How can you tell what it is *really* like to work in a school? Not by reading Ofsted reports or the school website; these will not reveal what it is like as a teacher on a daily basis in that particular school. This is because each school is completely bonkers. It is its own little world, complete with customs, behaviours and people. The secret to being happy as a teacher is to find the bonkers community that is *your* type of bonkers, where you look around the staff room and you think, 'They're all barking mad. But they are my kind of people and I belong here.' There can be nothing so lonely, particularly in small primary schools, as a staff that 'get each other' or buy into a culture, but you completely do not get it. That is not to say you have to be clones of each other; community does not mean all being the same. Instead, community means hearing and understanding differences and living happily with these differences. However, sometimes differences can just be too big. Furthermore, how are the staff treated, nurtured and developed? Some schools can be very different from others in this regard, and the same school can change over time, it is not static. You can of course go for a walk around the school, read the website and read the Ofsted report, as mentioned before, but these quite often tell you about the pupil/parent experience and not the staff one. Instead, what supply teaching offers you is the opportunity to experience a school from the inside as a member of staff. This gives you a 'try before you buy option' and, in fact, you can choose not to buy. In the same way, schools have the opportunity to 'try before they buy' with supply teachers, often requesting the same supply teacher that they hold in high regard to come in to provide cover. Furthermore, the second gift of supply teaching is that you can observe many different styles and forms of teaching and organising the learning environment, and if you are savvy you will 'nick a bit' of each one. By 'borrowing' the best of the vast array of ideas that you find, you will help to develop your very own unique blend. Last but by no means least, should you wish, you can go on holiday in term time. Of course, you do not get paid for the school holidays like teachers with full-time contracts, but then neither do you have to base your life around them, when activities are busy and holidays are full price.

Many student teachers will gain successful employment in a school that they are happy in for many years, perhaps this has been a placement school when training or perhaps this is a school that is known to them personally. Hopefully, this section has removed some of the perceived 'stigma' that surrounds supply teaching, as it can be a very savvy move for teachers embarking on their careers to 'go on supply' first. You can seek varied practice and really get to know different schools and what it is *really* like to work there. This will enable you to truly find a good fit for many years to come. If you are not convinced that supply teaching is worth it (simply for the cheaper holidays if nothing else) then the next section looks at considering when vacancies are likely to come out, where they can be found and what headteachers look for in an application.

JOB VACANCIES

Job vacancies for teaching tend to come out, in the main, three times a year. This is because teachers are expected to leave their positions at the end of one of the three school terms: Autumn, Spring and Summer. As teachers need to give two months' notice, the dates you could expect to see jobs advertised are as follows. For Autumn term, the day of departure would be 31 December so the last day of notice would be 31 October. For the Spring term, the day of departure would be 30 April, so the last day of notice would be 28 (or 29) February. Finally, for the Summer term, the last day of departure would be 31 August, making the last day of notice 31 May. Of course, as the dates listed above are the latest date a teacher could resign from their post this means that jobs may be advertised earlier.

The next consideration is where are jobs advertised? Teaching jobs are often advertised on the local council website for the school and with supply agencies (particularly for short-term cover), as well as on the school web-site, the new DfE teacher vacancy website, in national newspapers (particularly for overseas postings) and on other Internet sites. It can be worth considering where you would like to work before looking for jobs. One of the ways in which you can manage this is to consider, with a map, the distance and travel time you are willing to commute each day to work. Do note, however, that while some places are indeed further away, if they are on a quiet road for example, you may find that it is considerably quicker to commute there than it would be to go a shorter, busier route. Once you have worked out your travel radius, then you can start to make a list of the councils that operate in these areas. Start to check their websites; some websites will allow you to sign up to job feeds which would alert you when vacancies come out, while with others you will need to regularly check if there have been any developments.

When job adverts are posted, they tend to come with an overall description of the school and the post (job description), a person specification and key duties. In most cases, you will then be invited to attend a walk around the school and, if you like the setting, to then complete an application form and a personal statement/letter to the school. The application form, while a little tedious, should not present too many challenges, and most of these are completed online these days, so you can easily check your spelling and punctuation. However, do note, some areas are incredibly competitive for jobs, and so head-teachers often look for 'excuses' to make their enormous pile of applications smaller. Rejecting applications with simple grammar, punctuation and spelling mistakes can be an easy way of doing this. Remember to activate your spelling and grammar software and do not ignore any red or blue underlining of words or sections on your form.

The personal statement/letter can be a little bit trickier. This is how you can differentiate yourself from the other candidates and, in very base terms, clearly explain why a school should pay *you* a salary and not the other applicants, what you can bring, offer and 'do' that others cannot. How, then, should you approach writing your personal statement letter? The first task is to do your research. You need to understand two things: what the school is looking for (see person specification form) and what the school is 'about'.

First, then, is the person specification. This will detail what the essential skills/knowledge and attributes are for the job, as well as what the desired attributes are. Many sorting panels when reading applications will sit with a grid in front of them, which lists these essentials and desirables. They will then cross-reference the applications that they read, and sift those who meet the criteria into the shortlist panel. Therefore, you need to consider carefully what each school is looking for. Simply writing a generic letter and sending this out to all schools, irrespective of criteria, will not be successful. Of course, this takes much less time than crafting individual letters, but you will find that you are not as successful. This does not mean that you need to start completely from scratch each time, but you should edit, adapt and delete parts to make it tailored to each setting and each person specification. It can be useful to consider what the key topics of each of your paragraphs in your letter will be. You could group the specification attributes to form each paragraph; in fact this may already be done for you on the person specification. Many (although not all) group the attributes they are looking for under: qualifications and training, experience, knowledge and understanding, and personal qualities. Now, it would not be a particularly readable letter if you simply listed how you could demonstrate each attribute, and so the skill comes in constructing the letter to provide examples of what you did and the outcomes this had, which doesn't read like a list. In the first instance, it may actually be useful to just insert sentences to 'evidence' each attribute in your key paragraphs, and then once they're all evidenced you can go back and edit and rework to make it readable.

Then the next step is key. While you want the job and you are referencing your attributes, you need to keep firmly in mind that this is not all about you. In fact, this is about the school and the children that you are applying to teach. As such, you need to ensure that you understand the school, its policies and ethos. You should read the school website and any linked documentation, check if the school has a Twitter profile and consider latest Ofsted report. This will enable you to understand what complementary skills you can offer to the school. For example, if the school has a strong learning outside of the classroom ethos, and you are Forest School trained, this would be an important skill to make reference to, which will also ensure that you do not simply offer what is already catered for in the school. Once you have 'done your homework' you need to ensure that you are addressing the letter to the current headteacher. Sounds simple, and yet many trainees are caught out by this. As you can imagine, an incorrectly addressed letter is only going to end up in one place: the reject pile. Finally, after going through the above process, each time, for each school, while on placement, completing academic work and maybe working part time, the chances are that you will be sick of the sight of it and also too close to see any errors. Either give your letter to a trusted friend to review or use the careers service which is offered by your university, something that trainee teachers can overlook. Some of these services will let you submit the job description, person specification and your letter, and they will offer some critical feedback.

Many students now keep an Instagram profile as a log of their teaching and learning activities, and make reference to this in their letters of application. This allows prospective headteachers to view displays, resources and marking that trainees have been engaged in during their teaching placement. This is an interesting idea but one which is not to be entered into lightly. Firstly, your personal profile and your professional one should be so distant that no one can connect the two. The chances are that you will be fine at doing this; however, problems often arise if personal friends comment on professional profiles, and then through one link you appear in their pictures in a non-professional way. Secondly, all information about schools and children must be anonymised. Finally, having reviewed a number of sites over the years, it would appear that trainee teachers can blur or become confused about what is professional. For example, is a picture of your dog professional? Is a themed school day outfit selfie, complete with pout, professional? Is a meme referencing how tired you are professional? Almost every profile I have ever seen does not struggle with the 'big' stuff, e.g. no posts of nights out or hangovers, but many do introduce an element of the personal, which is actually not required for the purposes of a professional profile. It might be that folk who do this are trying to introduce an element or a flavour of themselves; however, the aim of one of these professional sites is to showcase your practice rather than you as a person and it is worth remembering this if you do post.

WORKING ABROAD

When you complete your teacher education course you may have your sights set on further afield and wish to apply for jobs abroad. This is a very interesting pathway to take and it is certainly worth doing your research properly before you accept a contract. The first thing to consider are the customs and practices of the country that you are looking at working in, as some of these may have a bearing on whether you can drink alcohol, or on your personal freedoms (particularly as a woman), or there may be other considerations for your particular lifestyle, such as having visible tattoos or being gay or a vegetarian. Some countries cater well for certain lifestyle choices; for example, in Taiwan, many Buddhists do not eat meat and so there are a variety of vegetarian restaurants (just look for the lotus sign). However, in some countries such as France, although times are changing, being a vegetarian can be a confusing lifestyle choice. There may be environmental and weather considerations such as earthquakes and monsoons, or just some great, but massive spiders knocking around. Some countries are very safe with low crime rates, but have high incidences of traffic accidents, while others may have a completely different profile. Do not assume that you know what a country is like, make sure to do your homework.

At the time of writing, the British Foreign Office provides travel advice for 225 countries/territories and structures (BFO, 2019). This information can be found under the following headings: Summary; Safety and security; Terrorism; Local laws and customs; Entry requirements; Health; Natural disasters; Money; Travel advice help and support. Once you have ascertained if the country you are considering working in is a good fit for you it is worth considering the school that you are applying for. British Overseas Schools are probably the gold standard of teaching jobs abroad, and you can find a list of accredited schools on the Department for Education's website. These schools operate an English Curriculum and tend to have good expat packages for staff. However, this is not to say that you cannot find a good and enjoyable job elsewhere or that a job you were successful in securing would be 'trouble free', but they are a good marker.

If you are researching a particular school, an interesting way to find information is to consider joining one of the expat websites and asking the community there for information; this should start to give you a feel for how the school is regarded in the expat community. Most expat communities are relatively small and, as such, everyone tends to be familiar with the schools. The *Times Educational Supplement* is the main place where overseas postings are advertised, and you can search by sector or by location. Applying for a job overseas is a leap into the unknown, and should not be entered into lightly. However, penalty clauses in contracts notwithstanding, if you get there and you find that you do not like it, you can always return home, and at least you will know that you've tried it, which is much better than spending the rest of your life regretting not going, or wishing you had been brave enough to try it. Do bear in mind though that there is a well-known phenomenon called culture shock. Culture shock does not tend to affect you the minute you land; this is because you are far too excited and everything is so novel. No, the 'crash' can come after a couple of months once everything has settled down, and those customs and cultures that you found initially 'interesting' start to really 'grate' on you. However, as with most things, being aware of this process is the first step and then knowing that 'this too shall pass' is also important. Drawing on your network of expat friends and the community can be important at this point, as can links with back home. Finally, do not expect schools in the UK to appreciate or understand what exactly you were doing out in Thailand or China or Qatar for three years. Some schools hear 'foreign destination' and think 'holiday', although this too is changing. Consider how you can use your experiences abroad to enhance your professional profile, for example by studying the language, which you can then offer to teach in school when you return. That is, if you ever decide to come back. A section of teachers enjoy it so much that they remain abroad.

PLACEMENT

PARENTS' EVENING

Learning to speak with and to pupils can initially be daunting; however, the prospect of speaking to parents can be even more troublesome for trainee teachers. This can often stem from feeling that 'you are not a proper teacher' and that the parents of your pupils will be able to see right through you. It is reasonable to say that parents and actually all people do make assumptions, correctly or incorrectly, about people when they meet them for the first time. However, you do have the chance to influence some of these assumptions to an extent. One of the first considerations is your professional appearance. You know the old saying, if it looks like a duck, it walks like a duck, and it probably is a duck. The same can be said for teachers. Consider the teachers you have at your placement. Do they all follow a 'professional look', which differentiates them from other staff in the school? Can you identify the teachers from their 'professional look' alone? If so, you need to look like a duck from the start. The next consideration is the language, tone and mannerisms that are used in your school, which vary from school culture to school culture but can be worth considering. Finally, try to be visible before parents' evening. Make sure that you send homework out, speak to parents when required or interact with them at school events. This means that you are not meeting the parents for the first time at parents' evening, but instead you are an accepted part of the teaching team.

It is important to realise that no one will know the pupils as well as their parents, therefore it is important to ensure that you understand who each child is and you are knowledgeable about their learning. The class teacher will lead the conversations with the parents and your role will most likely be that of an observer. However, if you have been working closely with a pupil or a group of pupils, then it is a reasonable expectation that you contribute to conversations where appropriate. If you are not sure what will be expected of you during parents' evening, then do make sure that you have an explicit conversation with your teacher about roles so you can prepare some information about certain children you have been working with if required. Talking about the wrong child or giving incorrect information to a parent can erode the trust that parents have in you as a professional. So if you are given a 'speaking role' at parents' evening it is important that you prepare or research what you will say. You may wish to run this by your teacher to ensure that you are both on the same page.

Using simple communication skills, such as making eye contact and a having relaxed body posture, is key in these situations, which is probably easier said than done. However, if you are explicitly aware of these things then at least if you find yourself with your arms folded, staring at the floor wishing it would swallow you up you can self-correct and refocus on the parents attending the meeting.

MENTAL HEALTH AND WELLBEING

'I'VE GOT 99 PROBLEMS, BUT SCHOOL HOLIDAYS AIN'T ONE'

Trainee teachers are very good at managing a diverse portfolio of tasks and people. They are usually great at managing pupils, their own families and their workload. Sometimes they are not always as great at managing themselves and their own emotions. And most commonly they worry. They worry about themselves, their pupils, their friends, their work, their teaching and occasionally, when they find a little respite, they can worry about not worrying. This section looks at worrying/anxiety, considers what is in the realms of 'normal' and tries to reframe this for you and contextualise it within your teacher training journey. However, before we start it is important to note that this chapter looks at supporting students who do not have an anxiety diagnosis, such as: generalised anxiety disorder; obsessive-compulsive disorder; panic disorder; post-traumatic stress disorder (PTSD); social phobia (or social anxiety disorder). If you are worried or concerned that you may be experiencing any of these anxiety disorders it is important that you seek help from your GP as soon as possible. You may also like to read *Anxiety for Beginners* by Eleanor Morgan (2016). This is not a medical book, although it is well informed. It is instead one woman's anxiety journey, and what is important to take from this is that she did not always receive the 'best' treatment at the outset. She had to ask, explore and try a variety of different forms of support and this is paramount to note. Sometimes, trainees will manage to find time to engage with support, which when they try it is not appropriate for them. However, sometimes they will then disengage with all other forms of support, feeling that each one would just be a waste of time and not helpful, like the one they have already tried.

ANXIETY

One of the most common issues for a trainee teacher is anxiety. Anxiety comes in all forms, and by this it is meant that sometimes anxiety is the correct response to a situation. For example, if you have an exam or a school interview then anxiety (provided it is within your parameters of 'normal') is the 'right' response. An unusual response to these life events would be delight and pleasure, which in my role looking after trainee teachers I think I would find even more troubling than when faced with a worried student. Another common anxiety-inducing task is essay writing. Again, some level of anxiety is normal, and actually quite helpful, because it is this feeling of worry/ being uncomfortable that motivates you to go and do something, for example some research. However, increasingly I have noticed that this anxiety, if not appropriately managed, can cause two much less helpful side effects: either misdirected anger/complaints against academic staff for insufficient academic support or a complete inability to focus on breaking down the task into manageable chunks to then action, as the student is completely overwhelmed by worry. Let us take each one in turn.

ITE lecturers used to be teachers. In addition, you know teachers by now; no one gets into it for the fame, glamour or monetary reward. Instead, teachers (maybe there is the odd rogue one in the mix) are motivated by helping people to learn, to develop their students and help them to achieve their best. In higher education a large part of this is through helping you achieve the academic component to your degree, and this is done through assignment support. You may also be interested to know that the NSS (National Student Survey – a nationally published survey for undergraduate students' 'satisfaction') and the PTES (Postgraduate Taught Experience Survey – a nationally published survey for postgraduate students' 'satisfaction') both have questions pertaining to student support for assessment. These two surveys act as extrinsic motivation for teaching staff to ensure that they fully support students with their assessments. What I am trying to highlight here is that as far as assessments go, it really is important that you and your tutors are on the same team. It is in no one's best interests for you to be unclear and unsure of what to do for an assignment. However, what they will not do is to write your assignment for you. There is only so much support that a tutor can provide, and the rest is up to you. This means that they will never tell you exactly what to do, because there are literally a million and one ways you could write your essay and all of them would meet the learning outcomes for the module. Therefore, this means that they will never remove all of your assessment anxiety because there will still be some considerations and problems for you to work out, and this is a 'normal' part of the process.

Over the past ten years higher education institutions have started to provide far more guidance and sessions on assignments than previously, and yet students are increasingly worried and want more and more. This might be due to the ever increasingly high stakes and competitive environments they have grown up in and experienced through the education system. That and the fact that each year of a university degree now costs at least £9,000 (without add-ons like accommodation) means that students are keen to obtain that all-coveted 2:1 or 1st class honours degree. And rightly so, but the way in which you manage yourself through this process is important and being aware of this 'bigger' picture that I have tried to outline is important. This is because sometimes a process or a task can be hard, or difficult or unpleasant, but that does not make it someone's fault. Being worried about something does not indicate that something is necessarily 'wrong', and it is important for you to try to assess your situation and ascertain if it is your reaction or your management of worry that is the concern. One of the best ways to do this is to commit all of your worries about something, particularly an assignment, onto paper. That way you can see in black and white what is concerning you.

CATEGORISING WORRIES

In general, your worries can be classified into two different groups: Type 1 worries (worry about future events) and Type 2 worries (worry about worry). I will focus on Type 1 worries here. Type 1 worries are grouped around things that may (or may not) happen in the future. These can then be further subdivided into current problems and hypothetical situations. The thing to note here is that current problems, happening here and now, are worries that you can do something about. However, hypothetical worries are actual worries that you cannot take any course of action to influence, alter or change but you can learn to react differently to these. Butler and Hope (2007) developed a flow process by which you can begin to tackle your Type 1 current problems, called the Worry Tree; if you search for this online you will be able to find many different models. However, the main idea of all of these is that you start at the top of the tree with noticing the worry. The anxiety or worry does not always manifest itself as such on a teacher training course straight away. Many students actually present in my office with anger, and when we sit down to unpick this, actually, at the back of most students' concerns is anxiety. In fact, many people resort to anger in order to protect themselves from acknowledging other more vulnerable feelings. In this way, anger can be described as a secondary emotion as we usually feel another emotion first before becoming angry. Learning to identify anxiety is an important key step. Then the next steps are almost as important. This is because the next steps help you to begin to manage the anxiety that you are feeling. Some students will simply state that they have 'anxiety' and leave it there; however, identification is the first step.

Ask yourself what you are worrying about. Is this a current worry or one that you are concerned about in the future? This is where most trees branch off in two directions, following the current worry pathway or the hypothetical worry pathway. We are going to consider the hypothetical one first as this is the shortest. If you realise that your worry is indeed hypothetical and as such you cannot do anything about it, then you need to, in the words of Elsa, let it go, change your attention focus. This requires practice and discipline. However, just as it is possible to learn anything new with patience and practice, so too is it possible to start to deal with hypothetical worries.

Current worries, those that you can do something about, require more consideration; in fact, they need an action plan. This looks at what the worry is made up of, how you plan to address it and when. You then have the choice of whether this action plan should be carried out now or later. If it can be dealt with now, then do it. Get that worry sorted, take the action you need to and let it go. This might be reading a journal article, it might be planning your introduction for an essay, but once you have made a start, then these worries start to go. If it is a worry that will need dealing with later, then make sure that you get out your diary or planner and you schedule it in, and then stick to it. In the in-between time, let it go and change focus, as there is nothing more you can do. Then when the time comes, action it.

Trainee teachers might be more prone to experiencing high levels of worry because they are faced with the double whammy of being a higher education student and out on placement developing as a teacher (nursing courses show similar anxiety levels among their students). As a trainee teacher you are learning what you do not know in university and receiving feedback, while also 'performing' and being visible all the time on placement. In addition, make no mistake about it, teaching is a performance sport, you do not have the sanctuary of retreating to a desk cubical and learning your craft alone, behind a screen where no one can find you. You learn in front of other adults and the pupils you are teaching. Therefore, the complete experience might feel like there is no respite. It is not really helped by the fact that most of your family and friends might not really understand 'what all the fuss is about' as surely your half days (at university or until 3.30 p.m. in school) are spent either 'dossing' or playing with kids. However, as with much in this book, acknowledging these issues of power and control and being so visible is important. Acknowledging these issues in a public space provides legitimacy for how you are feeling and the impact it has on you. Therefore, you should note that you're pretty awesome and this should always be your starting point. You are doing it: the teaching, the learning, the planning and the handing out of wet paper towels, irrespective of medical emergency. Moreover, once you have been kind to yourself, it is then time to look at how you could manage yourself even better by following a process such as the Worry Tree. You will not see success overnight. If you have been a worrier for years, you have to accept that it is going to take a little while to change your thinking, but if you never start the process, you will never see a change. And frankly, what have you got to lose? Yes. That is right, all those worries, which weigh you down and live in your head rent free. Evict them, you are far too busy. Instead, make room for some lightness, daydreaming and fantasies (of whatever flavour you find you have the energy for). After all, you only get one life, so try not to waste it worrying about things, which may or may not happen.

CHAPTER SUMMARY

- Supply teaching can really be a gift. Do not simply rule it out.
- Personalise your personal statement.
- Cross-reference your application with each and every person specification, skills and knowledge.
- Participate in parents' evenings, even if it is just making eye contact and welcoming parents.
- Do not allow worries to overtake your life: break them down, categorise them and either take action or let them go.

FURTHER READING

Devon, N. (2018) *A Beginner's Guide to Being Mental*. London: Bluebird.

An A–Z (from anxiety to zero f**ks given) by Natasha Devon is an interesting first introduction to many common metal health issues, complete with illustrations, which are quite funny. On a side note, Natasha was once the government's tsar for mental health, until she told them that the real issue for children in schools was the government's testing and accountability climate. Then she was 'let go'. However, she campaigns tirelessly around the country on behalf of young people regarding a variety of mental health issues.

Lonely Planet (2014) *The Best Place to Be Today: 365 Things to Do and the Perfect Day to Do Them*. Victoria, Australia: Lonely Planet Publications.

If you have the time, the passion and the money then this Lonely Planet guide is for you. Some are far, some are near, but none is as close to my heart as bog snorkelling in Llanwrtyd Wells, Powys (recommendation for 31 August). In 2014, I was the World Champion Female Bog Snorkelling Triathlete, but before you get too excited there were only two of us in the race! There are many other titles up for grabs (see Green Adventures website), just choose your race carefully. When I went back to defend my title there were five of us that year, and I didn't even come second.

Reader's Digest (2006) *The Most Amazing Places to Visit in Britain*. London: Reader's Digest.

This book has lots of lovely colour pictures and recommendations of places to go. Get a copy and put it on your desk when you work. It will remind you that life has so much to offer and adventures can be found just around the corner from wherever you live. Get your wellies/coat/suncream/umbrella/sunglasses/all of the above and get out, go see things and get inspired. Life is just too short to work and worry all the time.

8

FURTHER STUDY, TEACHING OUTSIDE THE CLASSROOM AND LOOKING AHEAD TO YOUR NQT YEAR

This
CHAPTER
EXPLORES:

- different study options at the end of your teacher training course, including studying abroad
- why you should take learning outside of the classroom and how to handle it
- the rare privilege of being a teacher and having pupils under your care, and why the world needs you as a teacher.

ACADEMIC

EXPLORING FURTHER STUDY OPTIONS

There can be very few things as unappealing as signing up to study an MA or other postgraduate courses in education the year after you graduate. In fact, what keeps many trainee teachers going is the knowledge that they will never need to study again. However, further study is often enjoyable or at least nowhere near as bad as your initial teacher education. Of course, when compared to a day out at a theme park or a night out with friends, undertaking further study is never going to compare. Although, when compared with what you have already completed, actually, in the grand scheme of things, it could be described as not that bad. There are a number of positives, which should now be considered before you completely dismiss further study and these are: an increasingly MA-based profession, 'being in the habit' and fees discounts.

There has been a drive, over the past ten years or so, to increase the number of teachers who hold Master's qualifications. There are a number of reasons for this push, including the belief that better-informed/qualified teachers can have more impact in the classroom. Especially since you consider that many education Master's degrees are aimed at practising teachers, and as such look at exploring and improving their classroom practice rather than just being a theoretically based study. Such degrees usually have titles such as Master's in Educational Practice or Master's in Advanced Educational Practice. These degrees focus on your practice in school and may incorporate action research to improve this using literature, theory and reflection. Sometimes, and perhaps that should read occasionally, given the financial constraints more and more schools are facing, schools will pay for such an MA or at least part of it, if the focus of your studies/research is a priority for the school. For example, if you wanted to make the business case for being funded/part-funded by your school you could chose as a topic the School Improvement Plan and other associated documents, and use this as a guide to your proposed study. You have certainly nothing to lose and you would not be tied into such a topic should your school decide not to fund you, so it is certainly worth a shot. More recently, there have been a selection of Master's in Mental Health degree courses validated. These are 'general' Master's degrees, which usually allow the students to choose two options to specialise in, such as mental health and the family or mental health and the school. Again, you might like to consider making the business case to your employing school about the school-wide benefits to having a member of staff who is both research active in this area and also perhaps investigating how to improve the mental health of teachers or a group of pupils. Of course, care should be taken not to 'over-egg it'. I have seen so many titles of MA research projects that could actually be several PhDs' worth. However, considering the specific needs of a specific group and investigating these is a reasonable task, and something that reflective teachers do naturally, and so you would simply be formalising this process.

In addition to teaching being an increasingly MA-based profession, another driver to the MA upskilling could be said to be the PISA tests. To understand the link between teachers' MAs and the PISA tests, the first point to be aware of is that for many years Finland was held as a paragon of education, in the international education ranking tables, and that the majority of Finnish teachers hold Master's degrees. Now it is at this point that this section is going to take a little diversion from Master's degrees to just explore the PISA test and Finland's education system. It's appropriate to you as teacher to understand a few international drivers and also to learn to ask questions about ideas and situation that are often presented in overly simplistic ways.

PISA TESTS

So what are PISA tests? It stands for the Programme for International Student Assessment (PISA), which is a survey undertaken every three years by the Organisation for Economic Co-operation and Development (OECD). The ultimate aim of PISA is to provide comparisons across global education systems. This is achieved by testing 15-year-olds. The scheme started in 2000 and over ninety countries participate. In England, the results are often presented in a ranking format with an indignant headline usually but not limited to such ideas as 'UK children slip down the internal rankings in X' or 'UK lags behind in global rankings'. That said, there was recently one headline which proclaimed that the UK was no longer stagnant, but stable, so perhaps in the next PISA results a new, more positive set of headlines may be found? Anyway, headlines aside, what you tend to find is that politicians will harness these results for their own political or party gain, declaring that 'the old ways don't work' and this is why they need to implement their own educational policies.

Another common phenomenon is that politicians, and the media to a lesser extent, focus on one aspect of another country's education system or policy and try to extrapolate this one aspect to their own education system, by suggesting that if in England we all just did X, then it would solve all educational issues. However, life is sadly often more complex than this and simply trying to transpose one aspect from a very different societal, cultural and wider educational context into another education context often does not work. For example, let us take a very quick look at some of the key aspects of Finland's education system. Finland's is an interesting example to consider because for some years it held the top spot of the PISA rankings, though more recently it has been 'overtaken' by some of the Asian countries such as Singapore, Japan and Taiwan. As a side note, Taiwan, in the rankings, is referred to as Chinese Taipei, and while this is certainly a conversation for another place and time, you may wish to conduct your own reading around Taiwan's current (precarious?) situation. You may also wish to note that Taiwan has never been Chinese, it has been Portuguese for example, and also under Japanese rule, but never Chinese.

Anyway, back to Finland, where there are very few non-public schools, so most of the population attend a 'normal' school. This means that the selection, removal and 'ghettoisation' of schools does not exist, as children from all walks of life attend the local school. Of course local housing allocation and prices do affect school intakes, but in theory at least there is a more equal intake. Furthermore, in these schools there are no nationalised standardised tests (National Matriculation Exam excepted) and there is less accountability to central government compared with England. Instead, teachers are charged with completing their own assessment, there is a focus on wellbeing and equality, pupils all receive free school meals, and there is easy access to health care, which includes psychological counselling. However, what does this all mean for teaching becoming a Master's-based profession, you may well be wondering. Well, the answer is that Finland's success in the PISA rankings, particularly about a decade ago, seemed to 'kick start' the drive in England for teaching to become an MA-based profession, with the over-simplistic link being made between Finland's educational success and all their teachers holding MAs. However, as noted before, simply taking one aspect of a very different context and transferring it to another context, such as England, may not have the direct results that are hoped for. In conclusion, and Finland aside, studying for an MA does empower you as a teacher. Undertaking an MA is a choice, rather than a necessity, and this places the teacher in a different 'head space'. As an MA student, you often have the freedom to choose your own area of study, directed to what you are passionate about. As a result of this choice and focus on investigating practice, quite often MA teacher students engage more with the process. This creates confidence and teachers who can critically reflect on their practice and have the gravitas, conferred by obtaining an MA, to share this with other teachers and professionals.

WHY STUDY AN MA?

There are two main reasons why you should start your MA as soon as you can after completing your initial teacher education. These two reasons are: 'being in the habit' and fees discount. 'Being in the habit' of reading, planning and writing assignments cannot be overestimated. Imagine it as training for a marathon. Over the course of your initial teacher training, you have put in hours of practice and now, unlike when you started, you have developed the stamina to teach and complete academic work. It should be acknowledged that this is not easy, but your skills, abilities and stamina have developed and quite frankly if this process were a sporting event, it would not be a jog, or even a 5k run. We are certainly talking Iron Man triathlon standard. However, as with all habits, when you stop performing them you lose the ability to undertake them, just like if an athlete stops training. It is easier to continue to study and teach, than to take five years off and try to restart. If MA study is what you want to eventually achieve, then you need to realise that there will never be a time you want to write an essay at the weekend or in the evening. Not ever. And once you have realised this, instead of debating when, you might as well crack on with it, realising that study misery is temporary, but letters after your name are for ever. A very motivational tool is to consider how you would feel meeting up with a group of your friends from initial teacher training in ten years' time, and finding out that some of them have MAs and you do not, or applying for a job in the future and learning some of the applicants have MAs and you do not. If your reaction is more one of 'meh' than 'oohhh, I'd be hopping mad with professional jealousy' then I suspect that MA study is not for you, as you need a fierce internal drive to keep you going. Furthermore, there is absolutely nothing wrong with not having an MA; some of the best teachers I have ever met do not have one. However, if you are interested, then most universities will offer a 15–20 per cent discount to students who return to study a postgraduate course the next year after graduating.

As mentioned above, there will always be other things that you want to do, both for your teaching as well as in your personal life. It will never happen that in five years' time you are suddenly going to have an abundance of time; in fact you may well have less time, given that you tend to accumulate professional responsibilities as you progress through school. Never will you sit down and relish writing an essay on a Sunday, or transcribing interviews in your summer holidays, but an MA is mercifully short when compared with other qualifications. Furthermore, as you have a level of autonomy over what you choose to focus on, and it is usually linked to your practice, this intrinsic motivation can sustain you as you study. Finally, quite often the most difficult aspect of a decision is making it, and if you made it and really thought it was the wrong decision for you, you could always just give it up. I would never, ever have dreamed of undertaking MA study – I simply did not feel 'bright enough'. I was lucky enough that my university was offering two modules from the MA course for free, for the first ten people to sign up. As I had nothing to lose, I thought: why not? And against all my firmly held beliefs that I 'wasn't an MA sort of person', I really enjoyed it and also did really well. That one single decision changed the course of my life and has opened doors to other opportunities and really helped to develop a sense of confidence in myself. It was this experience that makes me passionate about encouraging and supporting others to undertake MA study, while at the same time realising that it will not be 'right' for everyone. However, sometimes you might see people who have lots of qualifications and just assume that it was easy or that they are 'just like that'. Sometimes, they are. Often, people make 'lucky' decisions, which they are not sure about at the time, and then have to graft. Maybe next time you are at your university you should ask your tutors how they got their MAs and see what they say.

PLACEMENT

LEARNING OUTSIDE THE CLASSROOM: WHY BOTHER?

Perhaps the first place to start when considering learning outside the class-room is what exactly is learning outside the classroom? Is it residential, outdoor activities, Forest/Beach School or simply going out into the school grounds to learn rather than remaining in the classroom? The simple answer is that it is all of these activities; however, sometimes the exploration of the school and local area can be overlooked, and instead learning outside the class-room can loom incredibly large in the trainee teacher's mind. Perhaps a trainee teacher may have heard of the term but may not really understand why it is of importance to themselves or their teaching and this, plus the prospect of addi-tional risk assessment paperwork, can put a teacher off for life. This section will look at why learning outside the classroom is important for both pupils and teachers. It will then consider how as a student teacher you could go about incorporating outdoor learning into your teaching by using the school grounds in your training year.

Learning outside the classroom has gained prominence again, after a slight period of decline post-2010, with companies such as Persil becoming involved through the #embracedirt campaign encouraging children to go outside more. But why is learning outside the classroom such a big deal? There are many answers to this, including: providing real world experiences through investigations and experimental learning, developing a respect and enjoyment of being outdoors, and enhancing the different dynamics of children's relationships between themselves as well as with the teacher. In fact, there is a chapter by Simon Catling (2014) in the fantastic book *Learning to Teach in the Primary School* (this chapter is of interest to secondary colleagues too, so don't be off put by the book title), which details all of these values in much greater depth than will be covered here, and also links to the research papers from which they came, should you wish to conduct further research. However, there are also three more recent considerations, which deserve consideration. The first consideration concerns the amount of time that children now spend outside, which has decreased over the past decade (National Trust, 2019). Meanwhile, time spent watching TV (17 hours per week according to the National Trust) and engaging in activities online (more than 20 hours a week) has increased, with this being most pronounced in the 11–15 age range. This latter group, according to the National Trust, 'spend about half their waking lives in front of a screen: 7.5 hours a day, an increase of 40% in a decade' (2012: 4). Some parents have high levels of concern about their children playing outside the home, for reasons such as 'stranger danger' and abduction, or increased traffic risks on the roads. They feel instead that it is safer to have their children inside where they can control the environment. However, what some parents neglect to consider is that quite often they cannot control the environments to which their children are exposed to online.

The second more recent consideration is the publicised effects of climate change, and the speed at which it is taking place. Climate change and its effects are an important global issue that pupils should have an awareness of. Furthermore, if changes are to be made to the way we currently live in order to conserve and protect the Earth's resources and wildlife, then children need to grow up with an appreciation of the outdoors, in a variety of contexts. Otherwise, the risk becomes that 'nature' is just another thing to be consumed through TV or online, but not experienced or lived.

The third and final consideration is the wellbeing that being outdoors can provide for both teachers and students alike. The Japanese have been aware of the benefits of being outside for some time now and have a word to describe it, *shinrin-yoku*, while the term 'biophilia' (Wilson, 1984) has been used in England, although not very frequently. *Shinrin-yoku* translates as 'forest bathing'. It was developed in Japan during the 1980s and has become a cornerstone of preventive health care and healing in Japanese medicine. This concept seems to be making inroads into popular culture in England too. There is a podcast series on BBC Radio 4, called *Forest 404*, which as well as being a radio drama also plays the sounds of a forest. If you are interested, the drama is set in the twenty-fourth century where all forests have been wiped out. The lead character comes across audio recordings of sounds that cannot be identified, which are from forests, and she sets out to discover why forests no longer exist, all the time hunted down by the new world's ruling powers. It is an interesting format, because there are three aspects to each 'show'. There is the thriller (the drama as outlined above), the talks (discussions on the themes raised in each episode from a vast array of speakers) and the soundscapes ('immersive soundscapes of natural world environments, mixed in binaural for a 3D headphone experience … including the Sumatran Rainforest, the songs of whales, a chorus of frogs'). It may have crossed your mind that this is somewhat of a diversion from where we started (which seems to be an additional theme of this chapter) but ideas are often interconnected. The point is to draw your attention to what research shows: that simply listening to outdoor sounds can be beneficial to your wellbeing. This is useful to know for you, as a busy teacher, but also for your pupils' wellbeing too. However, listening to outdoor sounds is not shown to be as good as actually going outside, in fact as little as ten minutes outside per day, three times per week has been shown to reduce feelings of anxiety (Hunter, Gillespie and Chen, 2019). Wellness indicators show that teachers and their pupils are experiencing increasing difficulties with their mental health, and wellbeing is now firmly on schools' agendas. After all, what learning can take place without well (both physically and mentally) pupils and teachers? Therefore, it is important that as a trainee teacher you realise that you simply cannot be too busy to consider your students' and your own wellbeing. In fact, this is the cornerstone of learning, and unless you and your pupils are well, then learning will not take place to the extent to which it could.

When considering learning outside the classroom, for all pupils it is interesting to consider practice in the EYFS where daily use of the outdoor spaces, irrespective of weather, is planned into a child's learning experiences. However, sadly once these children enter Year 1 these outdoor experiences are more limited and by secondary school, unless it is a field trip or a PE lesson, in some schools going outside is simply not an option for many children. Teachers often feel that they do not have time in a busy curriculum to take the children outside. However, it is worth noting that learning outside of the classroom and curriculum learning do not necessarily exist in opposition. No extra time needs to be found if consideration is given to how learning from all subjects could be undertaken in the outdoor context, initially within the school grounds. If this approach is taken, while no extra time needs to be found, there is an initial outlay of time in terms of developing routines and expectations with your classes. For example, establishing a routine can take a little time and patience, to ensure that pupils gather what they need, leave the classroom in an orderly fashion and are in the right mindset for learning. This is important so that you do not disturb the whole school with a disruptive bunch of kids, who keep popping back to class for forgotten items, who think that they are in for a 'jolly'. However, it is more important to ensure that your pupils are ready to learn, and their time can be maximised.

So how as a trainee teacher can you start to plan teaching outside in your lessons? It is worth, in the first instance, discussing with your school mentor learning outside the classroom and what the school policy and procedures are for implementing this across the curriculum. Some schools are quite well developed in this area, carrying out what the Council for Learning Outside the Classroom (2018) call frequent, continuous and progressive learning outside the classroom experiences. While in other settings learning outside the classroom may be relegated to the once a year residential trip. Ensure that you read the school's policy covering this area as all contexts will be different. If your school does map learning outside the classroom across the year groups, then you will be able to adapt your planning to cater for these experiences. If, however, this is something which is not common, discuss with your teacher what lessons might be best suited to the outdoor learning context.

YOUR PUPILS' NEEDS

The age of the children in your class and the subjects that you are teaching will tend to lead your thoughts about learning outside the classroom. You should consider your lesson objectives, how being outside will enhance the learning for your students, but also consider how being outside might motivate your students. You then need to consider the needs of your pupils, and if going outside is inclusive and caters for their needs. For example, some children on the autistic spectrum may need advanced preparation and planning in the days leading up to going outside. If you use a visual timetable with such a student you may need to introduce the 'new card' representing learning outside the classroom and discuss with the child what this might look like. Another useful strategy, which caters for a variety of needs, are Social Stories. These are short descriptions of 'particular situations, events or activities, which include specific information about what to expect in that situation and why' (Gray, 1991). In many cases, if you make these stories yourself, you can include pictures of the child or the school grounds and be explicit about the behaviour and responses that you would like to have from the pupil(s). The secret to good learning outside the classroom experiences (for both you and the children) is forward planning, ensuring that as far as possible you try to anticipate and minimise disruption and risk, and maximise the learning time. It is not just children with additional needs or barriers to learning who benefit from a proactive approach to preparing for out of the classroom learning. In fact, there is an argument that all children could be prepared in advance, regarding the behaviour expectations and the learning that they will engage in. As a teacher, you will have considered how the learning meets the learning outcome for that lesson, and also how it fits into your series of lessons, but have you shared this with your pupils? Do they understand how the outdoor lesson fits with the teaching sequence and what they are expected to do with their new learning? To ensure motivation and relevance it is important that all of your pupils understand what they should do with the learning that they have conducted outside. If they are aware of how outdoor learning feeds into the next lesson, then it can help to stop the outside lesson from being considered a 'doss lesson' and provide it with status and importance. You also need to ensure that the learning 'briefing' is conducted in your classroom before you go outside; the last thing you want to be doing is shouting your learning instructions outside at a group of excited children because, let's face it, simply being outside is going to be much more exciting than anything that you have to say. Set it all up in advance, then when you get outside, all you will need is a few key reminders and off they go. You may also like to consider a mini-plenary sign/sound for outside and how you expect the children to respond, as well as a sign/sound for the end of the lesson. But what exactly do you need to set up? Ah, well, this all depends on what you are teaching the children, how old these pupils are and what their specific needs are. However, what will be outlined next are a couple of the main organisational ideas which you could adapt in the first instance of outdoor learning before you look at creating more bespoke ideas.

ORGANISATIONAL ISSUES

The first suggestion is that there are several stations already set up in the outdoor area, which maximise being outdoors. The pupils then rotate around each station, participating in the activity, experiment or learning experience that you have set up. You will need to consider how you want the children to record (if at all) their learning. Is it necessary to write this down? If so, consider how this will be achieved, through a worksheet on a clipboard, or through bringing their books outside? Or would it be more appropriate to use technology to record learning, such as cameras, video recording or dictaphones? Perhaps you would just like them to participate in the activities and when you come back to the classroom then you will start to record or discuss or build upon the learning outside. Another suggestion involves all the students working as a whole, so they are focused on the same task at the same time. Again, issues of recording need to be carefully considered, as does the area within which you are expecting them to work. With the carousel activity described above, it is clear where each child will be at each time and you can allocate your adult support appropriately. However, attention needs to be given to how you manage all children participating in the same activity at the same time. If you do have additional adults who work with your class, you might want to consider completing a separate outdoor lesson plan for them, which clearly outlines what their role is with regards to behaviour management of specific children or/and how they are expected to participate in the learning experience. For example, do you want them to take a small group, or would it be more helpful to have them floating around the activities that you have set up in advance? It may be that one group at a time are to go outside with a supporting adult to complete a specific task while you remain in the classroom working with the remaining pupils on a rotational basis.

When working within the school grounds you will not normally need to conduct a risk assessment, which makes it more accessible for the trainee teacher. However, you should make sure that you do a check of the parts of the school site that you want to use the morning before your lesson. This is just to ensure that there is nothing there from the night before, or the weekend if it is the start of the week. You can of course insert your own items here, but from experience you might want to start to consider looking for items such as dead pigeons, dog poo, condoms or glass bottles, which you would not want the students to encounter.

How you choose to organise your learning outside the classroom is not really important, as long as it enhances the learning for your pupils and is carried out in a safe and enjoyable manner for all, and this includes you. As with any aspect of teaching, it would be sensible to take the approach that you will learn as you go along, and so it is really important to discuss with your mentor any upcoming ideas or lessons as they may be able to predict possible issues that you may encounter. As an eager NQT, I took a group of children out to explore capacity, using large containers and lots of water, which simply would not have been possible in the classroom. My feedback was broadly positive, although it was pointed out to me that I had the children working in the only shaded part of the playground where teeth had been seen chattering at one point, and I was asked why I had not moved the children into the sunshine. This was a fair and reasonable comment; my only answer was that I had been so focused on behaviour management and enhancing learning that what could reasonably be referred to as common sense had left me. So, do make sure you seek advice from a more experienced teacher, because when you go outside, you have many things on your mind, and could easily overlook some simple aspects.

MENTAL HEALTH AND WELLBEING

LESSONS LEARNED: A REVIEW AND LOG READY FOR YOUR NQT YEAR

There will be moments in your initial teacher training when you feel that you are getting nowhere fast, that you are not improving and that it will simply never, ever end. And then all of a sudden, one year it will be Christmas and the next thing you know the children are making you leaving cards and you are snivelling into your cardigan. It is like this for most people. Moreover, even when you get that all-coveted for ever job, the September-to-December slog is akin to being in the trenches, but the next thing you are aware of is the disruption of summer exams and then it is the school play and the summer holidays. It has been considered in this book already, but simply being aware of these patterns and expectations can be helpful. This too shall pass.

This section considers what you have learned over your teacher training and how you can 'bank' it for when you need it as an NQT.

A TEACHER'S WORK IS NEVER DONE

As a teacher your work will never be done. In many jobs, when you clock off and go home you simply cannot take your work with you, but you now know as a teacher this in not the case. Furthermore, even if you did get to the end of a day's tasks, chances are all of these jobs will be back tomorrow.

For example, the marking of books and planning of lessons. There is a great saying that 'life isn't about waiting for the sunshine, it's about learning to dance in the rain'. You could easily replace this with, 'teaching isn't about finishing all of your jobs, it's about learning to have a life while doing them'. There is always a research paper you could be reading to inform your practice, a resource to be made, a more detailed comment to be given regarding a pupil's response to your initial marking, another extra-curricular club you could host, another assessment system to get to grips with and don't forget every couple of years the government *du jour* will have a complete and total overhaul of all you once knew and understood about education and teaching. Some trainee teachers find this difficult to manage. They like a to-do list to be completed, ticked and finished, not to keep expanding *ad infinitum*, but the chances are that having successfully completed your teacher training you are now a multi-tasking ninja. You know what is important to spend time on, and actually what corners you can legitimately cut without impacting on your pupils' learning. Well done, O Wise One. However, it might be that you are still carrying out some unnecessary tasks, or approaching tasks in a laborious manner. Which is completely to be expected as a new professional. However, what it does mean is that you should try to continue experimenting with your practice as you embark on the profession and consider what really makes a difference to pupils' learning and what does not. You may find yourself surprised and hopefully less burdened by 'busy' tasks or approaches to tasks which actually do not count.

NO ONE WILL EVER BE AS HARD ON YOU AS YOU

Teachers when asked at the end of a lesson, 'How do you think it went?', usually give a maximum of one positive aspect of their lesson followed by a flurry of things that could have been improved or aspects of the lesson that they would do differently. When trainee teachers receive their assignments back, unless they have received 100 per cent then there is that nagging feeling that they are 'just no good' or they are 'rubbish' and that 'black-and-white thinking' (which we looked at in Chapter 3) comes into play. However, over the course of the year, you come to realise (some sooner than others) that you are not rubbish, in fact you are pretty amazing. You are brilliant, because you now know you will have great lessons, and not so great lessons. You will have fantastic days and some pretty mediocre days; occasionally you'll have the sort of day where you should just go home, have a shower/bath, put on your PJs and simply write off the rest of the day and start again tomorrow. And this is all fine. It is more than fine because you now realise that you are a human being and not a robot. It is this humanness that makes you empathetic, creative and fun; all the things that pupils love in a teacher when they are learning. However, it also can make you prone to mistakes and a lack of consistency. Of course, you can easily fall into the 'I'm just no good' thinking trap, but hopefully you are aware of the pitfalls of black-and-white thinking, worrying about hypotheticals, being tired, not eating well, not going outside, or not doing any exercise.

Everyone's basic need to practise a self-care routine is different, and it would not do for us to all be the same. However, you need to be aware of what you need to do to keep well. Consider car maintenance as a helpful illustration. You make sure there is petrol in the tank, air in the tyres and the windows are clean. Furthermore, if there is a knocking or rattling sound you do not just ignore it, or it could be costly – you take it into a garage or you explore it yourself and address the problem while it is small, before it gets very expensive. Then once a year you take your car for an MOT. This is basically how you need to look after yourself. Although, too many teachers will simply run themselves into the ground, caring for others. Self-care is a priority not an option, and usually you know this by the end of your training year. Therefore, the key message here is to throw yourself wholeheartedly into your NQT year, or going on supply or whatever else you wish to do, but from time to time just be aware of how you are feeling and why. Chances are, sometime between September (ooh giddy, new class, new year) and the Christmas break (Sleep. I. Need. Some. Sleep) you might experience a little blip (my bet would be November – clocks have gone back, it's always dark, you are knackered, the next break is weeks away). Do not ignore this little blip, but consider if you are doing the things that keep you well and the answer will almost always be 'no', followed by 'I'm too busy'. See above, 'a teacher's work is never done'. However, you know now that this is a misdirection. You cannot be too busy to look after yourself, and generally if you take time, it makes time, as you can get through your jobs a little quicker and actually be more productive if you are feeling 100 per cent.

BEING A TEACHER IS SIMPLY BRILLIANT – UTTERLY KNACKERING BUT BRILLIANT

You are now aware of what keeps teachers working in a profession that is often not as well respected by the media or politicians and sometimes the general public as it should be. You now know that teachers are not in it for the money, or even the hours. You know it is simply because the ability to work with future generations, inspiring, shaping and sharing in their lives, is a privilege. You can watch the news and feel disheartened about climate change or people's ability to understand each other and then go to work and 'do something about it'. Educating children and enabling them to fulfil their potential is brilliant work. Those light bulb moments, when a pupil you are teaching finally understands a concept, are what keeps you going. Furthermore, no two days are ever the same. Who knows what is going to happen? And despite sometimes wishing that you might have two days that are the same, or longing for a desk job, a data-entry cubicle job, actually you know this would bore the pants off you and suck the life out of your soul. Yes, you will have to take the rough with the smooth: the child that does not listen, that class which is such hard work, the long hours and the endless marking. Overall, it is not a bad life and you'll certainly never, ever be bored. Finally, through working as a teacher over the years, you will become a 'Quiz Ninja', the person that everyone turns to if a proper answer needs to be found. You and you alone know the difference between weight and mass, you know the difference between 'their', 'they're' and 'there', and how many current planets there are in the Solar System. On a more serious note, the intrinsic value that you get from educating, caring for and developing young people simply cannot be replicated. For some children in your class, you will be their only constant, a safe person to talk to and a source of inspiration. Education has the power to change lives, and you are the person that delivers this. Through education children can grow to make more informed decisions, which affect their health and wellbeing and that of their future families and generations. Teaching helps to distribute wealth, opportunities and privileges within a society, contributing to social justice. It is for these reasons you now know you should be proud to be a teacher despite the fact it is utterly knackering.

CHAPTER SUMMARY

- Seriously consider studying for an MA. And don't leave it too long – it'll be harder and harder to come back to.
- Be interested and informed about the international educational perspective.
- Take learning outside: for you and for your pupils.
- However, if you are going outside you must be organised.
- Remember above all else you have the power to transform lives. To inspired, educate and provide a safe space for the children in your care is a rare privilege and as such being a teacher is simply the best job in the world. It's one of the most knackering but no other career gives the same rewards.
- So remember you're amazing and be kind to yourself as you go through your career. The world needs teachers like you.

FURTHER READING

Catling, S. 'Valuing, organising and managing learning outside the classroom', in T. Cremin and J. Arthur (eds) (2014) *Learning to Teach in the Primary School*, 3rd edition. London: Routledge, pp. 231–250.

In the fantastic book *Learning to Teach in the Primary School*, Simon Catling provides details and links to research papers for conducting successful and thoughtful learning outside the classroom.

Need a little teacher 'pick me up' inspiration and reminder of why you are so important? OK, then, here are four great teacher and teaching movies for you: *Akeelah and the Bee* (2006), *Dead Poets Society* (1989), *Karate Kid* (the 1984 one) and *School of Rock* (2003). Alternatively, if you need to feel like 'actually, I'm doing a fine job' then perhaps *Bad Teacher* (2011) and *Bad Education* (TV sitcom, 2012–2014) are for you.

REFERENCES

Barnes, J. (2015) *Cross-curricular Learning 3–14*, 3rd edition. London: Sage.

Bloom, B. S. (1956) *Taxonomy of Educational Objectives: The Classification of Educational Goals*. New York: Longmans, Green.

Blum, S, D. (2009) *My Word! Plagiarism and College Culture*. Ithaca: Cornell University Press.

Broadwell, M. M. (1969) 'Teaching for learning', *The Gospel Guardian*, 20(41): 1–3.

Brookfield, S. (2005) *Becoming a Critically Reflective Teacher*. San Francisco: Jossey Bass.

Bruner, J. (1986) *Actual Minds, Possible Worlds*. Cambridge, MA: Harvard University Press.

Buckler, S. and Castle, P. (2014) *Psychology for Teachers*, 2nd edition. London: Sage.

Catling, S. (2014) 'Valuing, organising and managing learning outside the classroom', in T. Cremin and J. Arthur (eds), *Learning to Teach in the Primary School*, 3rd edition. London: Routledge, pp. 231–250.

Chartered College of Teaching (2019) https://chartered.college/ (accessed 6 September 2019).

Clance, P. R. and Imes, S. A. (1978) 'The imposter phenomenon in high achieving women: Dynamics and therapeutic intervention', *Psychotherapy: Theory, Research & Practice*, 15(3): 241–247. http://dx.doi.org/10.1037/h0086006.

Cockburn, A. and Handscomb, G. (eds) (2012) *Teaching Children 3–11*, 3rd edition. London: Sage.

Cremin, T. and Arthur, J. (eds) (2014) *Learning to Teach in the Primary School*, 3rd edition. London: Routledge.

Cremin, T. and Burnett, C. (eds) (2018) *Learning to Teach in the Primary School*, 4th edition. London: Routledge.

Cuddy, A. (2012) 'Your body may shape who you are'. www.ted.com/talks/amy_cuddy_your_body_language_shapes_who_you_are?language=en (accessed 2 September 2019).

Denby, N. (ed.) (2015) *Training to Teach*, 3rd edition. London: Sage.

Devon, N. (2018) *A Beginner's Guide to Being Mental*. London: Bluebird.

DfE (Department for Education) (2011) *Teachers' Standards: Guidance for School Leaders, School Staff and Governing Bodies*, July 2011 (introduction updated June 2013). https://assets.publishing.service.gov.uk/government/uploads/system/uploads/attachment_data/file/665520/Teachers__Standards.pdf (accessed 4 September 2019).

DfE (Department for Education) (2013) *History Programmes of Study: Key Stages 1 and 2*. https://assets.publishing.service.gov.uk/government/uploads/system/uploads/attachment_data/file/239035/PRIMARY_national_curriculum_-_History.pdf (accessed 4 September 2019).

DfE (Department for Education) (2014) *Teachers' Workload Diary Survey 2013.* Research report, February 2014. https://assets.publishing.service.gov.uk/government/uploads/system/uploads/attachment_data/file/285941/DFE-RR316.pdf (accessed 4 September 2019).

DfE (Department for Education) (2016) *School Workforce in England: November 2015.* SFR 21/2016, 30 June 2016. https://assets.publishing.service.gov.uk/government/uploads/system/uploads/attachment_data/file/533618/SFR21_2016_MainText.pdf (accessed 4 September 2019).

DfE (Department for Education) (2018) *School Teachers' Pay and Conditions Document 2018 and Guidance on School Teachers' Pay and Conditions.* https://assets.publishing.service.gov.uk/government/uploads/system/uploads/attachment_data/file/740575/School_teachers__pay_and_conditions_document_2018.pdf (accessed 4 September 2019).

DfE (Department for Education) (2019) *Keeping Children Safe in Education: Statutory Guidance for Schools and Colleges.* https://assets.publishing.service.gov.uk/government/uploads/system/uploads/attachment_data/file/828312/Keeping_children_safe_in_education.pdf (accessed 4 September 2019).

EFF (Education Endowment Foundation) (2015) 'New £2M fund to find best ways to improve outcomes for EAL pupils'. https://educationendowmentfoundation.org.uk/news/new-2m-fund-to-find-best-ways-to-improve-outcomes-for-eal-pupils/ (accessed 5 September 2019).

Elsesser, K. (2018) 'Power posing is back: Amy Cuddy successfully refutes criticism', *Forbes*, 3 April. www.forbes.com/sites/kimelsesser/2018/04/03/power-posing-is-back-amy-cuddy-successfully-refutes-criticism/ (accessed 2 September 2019).

Gewirtz, S. (2013) 'Developing teachers as scholar-citizens, reasserting the value of university involvement in teacher education', in L. Florian and N. Pantić (eds), *Learning to Teach.* York: Higher Education Academy. www.heacademy.ac.uk/system/files/resources/learningtoteach_part1_final.pdf (accessed 4 September 2019).

Hunt, A., Burt, J. and Stewart, D. (2015) *Monitor of Engagement with the Natural Environment: A Pilot for an Indicator of Visits to the Natural Environment by Children – Interim Findings from Year 1* (March 2013 to February 2014). Natural England Commissioned Reports, NECR166.

Inclusion for All (2019) http://ww.inclusionforall.co.uk/ (accessed 6 September 2019)

Jubilee Centre (2018) University of Birmingham. www.jubileecentre.ac.uk/ (accessed 2 September 2019).

Knowles, G. and Holmstrom, R. (2013) *Understanding Family Diversity and Home–School Relations.* Abingdon: Routledge.

Knowles, G. and Lander, V. (2011) *Diversity, Equality and Achievement in Education.* London: Sage.

Kokkinos, C. M. (2011) 'Job stressors, personality and burnout in primary school teachers', *British Journal of Educational Psychology*, 77(1): 229–243.

MacBlain, S. (2014) *How Children Learn.* London: Sage.

Maslow, A. H. (1943) 'A theory of human motivation', *Psychological Review*, 50(4): 370–396.

Maslow, A. H. (1954) *Motivation and Personality.* Oxford: Harpers.

McKay, K. and McKay, B. (2018) 'How to quit mindlessly surfing the Internet and actually get stuff done', *The Art of Manliness*, 6 December. www.artofmanliness.com/articles/how-to-quit-mindlessly-surfing-the-internet-and-actually-get-stuff-done/ (accessed 2 September 2019).

Montessori, M. and Claremont, C. A. (1969) *The Absorbent Mind.* New York: Dell Publishing Co.

Morgan, E. (2016) *Anxiety for Beginners*. London: Bluebird.

Naz and Matt Foundation (2019) www.nazandmattfoundation.org/about/ (accessed 6 September 2019)

Pavlov, I. P. (1902) *The Work of the Digestive Glands*. Birmingham: Classics of Medicine Library.

Peters, S. (2012) *The Chimp Paradox*. London: Vermilion.

Piaget (1952) *The Origins of Intelligence in Children* (translated by M. Cook). New York: International Universities Press.

Piaget, J. (1958) 'The growth of logical thinking from childhood to adolescence', *AMC*, 10: 12.

Santrock, J. W. (2004) *Educational Psychology*, 2nd edition. New York: McGraw-Hill.

Schön, D. (1987) *Educating the Reflective Practitioner*. San Francisco: Jossey-Bass Publishers.

Sellars, M. (2014) *Reflective Practice for Teachers*, 2nd edition. London: Sage.

Seuss, Dr. (1990) *Oh, the Places You'll Go!* New York: Random House.

Skinner, B. F. (1938) *The Behavior of Organisms: An Experimental Analysis*. Oxford: Appleton-Century.

Stîngu, M. (2012) 'Reflexive practice in teacher education: Facts and trends', *Procedia – Social & Behavioural Sciences*, 33: 617–621.

Stonewall (2019) www.stonewall.org.uk/supporting-schools (accessed 6 September 2019)

Sweller, J. (1988) 'Cognitive load during problem solving: Effects on learning', *Cognitive Science*, 12(2): 257–285.

Tripp, D. (1993) *Critical Incidents in Teaching: Developing Professional Judgement*. London: Routledge.

TSC (Teaching Schools Council) (2016) *Effective Primary Teaching Practice 2016*. Available at: www.tscouncil.org.uk/wp-content/uploads/2016/12/Effective-primary-teaching-practice-2016-report-web.pdf (accessed 2 September 2019).

Vygotsky, L. S. (1978) *Mind in Society: The Development of Higher Psychological Processes* Cambridge, MA: Harvard University Press.

Watson, J. B. and Rayner, R. (1920) 'Conditioned emotional reaction', *Journal of Experimental Psychology*, 3: 1–14

Williams, J. (2018) *'It Just Grinds You Down': Persistent Disruptive Behaviour in Schools and What Can Be Done About It*. London: Policy Exchange. https://policyexchange.org.uk/wp-content/uploads/2019/01/It-Just-Grinds-You-Down-Joanna-Williams-Policy-Exchange-December-2018.pdf (accessed 2 September 2019).

INDEX